"Like a good physician, Meador offers penetrating yet accessible diagnoses and remedies for our contemporary milieu. Identifying the breakdown of our perception of the natural order in relation to ourselves, creation, and our neighbor, Meador draws from the broad Christian tradition (and heavy doses of Herman Bavinck) to offer concrete responses. This book thus challenges us because Christian discipleship involves radical self-giving and obedience. But it is also an invitation, for as Meador reminds us, we are never more natural than when we love."

N. Gray Sutanto, assistant professor of systematic theology at Reformed Theological Seminary, Washington, DC

"Jake Meador continues to give us an accessible but deeply informed account of what he calls 'Christian social doctrine.' He begins by contrasting late modernity's view of nature—as a place of chaotic power conflicts—with that of the magisterial Protestant Reformation—as a work of God's love. On the basis of this 'thick' conception of the natural order, he then insightfully shows how it provides an alternative, life-giving way to understand race, sex, technology, the family, the environment, politics, and institutions. Our polarized and fragmenting contemporary church needs this book!"

Timothy Keller, pastor emeritus, Redeemer Presbyterian Church of New York City

"A voice in the wilderness of current culture wars, Meador has written a provocative and unsettling Christian critique of modernity. Deftly incorporating an arresting selection of voices, many far too lightly dismissed by Christians as their ideological antagonists, Meador presents an inspiring, bracing, and rigorously orthodox vision of Christian life, thought, and community as a hopeful response to its challenges and possibilities."

Alastair Roberts, adjunct senior fellow, Theopolis Institute

"Meador's book is a call for a more rooted world in which Christians pursue justice, mercy, and holiness in a sphere that will not be tamed or controlled. Touching on race, gender, economics, ecology, and more, it is a vision that is both comprehensive and full, yet modest and grounded. In these pages, there is much to provoke and to challenge, as Meador offers a vision of the Christian's participation in the world, which is as small as the household and as sweeping as the cosmos."

Myles Werntz, associate professor of theology at Abilene Christian University

"A book that pairs a trenchant critique of whiteness guided by Willie Jennings with a robust Reformed orthodoxy guided by Herman Bavinck is precisely the book that I've been looking for. Meador's work is a text of truth, goodness, and beauty revealing to us the world in which we live and the way we ought to move about in it."

Malcolm Foley, director of Black church studies at Truett Seminary

FOREWORD BY
KAREN SWALLOW PRIOR

WHAT
ARE
CHRISTIANS
FOR?

LIFE TOGETHER *at the*
END *of the* WORLD

JAKE MEADOR

An imprint of InterVarsity Press
Downers Grove, Illinois

InterVarsity Press
P.O. Box 1400, Downers Grove, IL 60515-1426
ivpress.com
email@ivpress.com

InterVarsity Press® is the book-publishing division of InterVarsity Christian Fellowship/USA®, a movement of students and faculty active on campus at hundreds of universities, colleges, and schools of nursing in the United States of America, and a member movement of the International Fellowship of Evangelical Students. For information about local and regional activities, visit intervarsity.org.

Scripture quotations, unless otherwise noted, are from The Holy Bible, English Standard Version, copyright © 2001 by Crossway Bibles, a division of Good News Publishers. Used by permission. All rights reserved.

While any stories in this book are true, some names and identifying information may have been changed to protect the privacy of individuals.

The publisher cannot verify the accuracy or functionality of website URLs used in this book beyond the date of publication.

Cover design and image composite: David Fassett
Interior design: Daniel van Loon
Images: forest above city: © borchee / E+ / Getty Images
    old tree with sun rays: © dem-belitsky / iStock / Getty Images Plus
    paper texture: © Katsumi Murouchi Moment / Getty Images

ISBN 978-0-8308-4736-5 (print)
ISBN 978-0-8308-4737-2 (digital)

Printed in the United States of America ∞

InterVarsity Press is committed to ecological stewardship and to the conservation of natural resources in all our operations. This book was printed using sustainably sourced paper.

Library of Congress Cataloging-in-Publication Data
A catalog record for this book is available from the Library of Congress.

| **P** | 22 | 21 | 20 | 19 | 18 | 17 | 16 | 15 | 14 | 13 | 12 | 11 | 10 | 9 | 8 | 7 | 6 | 5 | 4 | 3 | 2 | 1 |
| **Y** | 40 | 39 | 38 | 37 | 36 | 35 | 34 | 33 | 32 | 31 | 30 | 29 | 28 | 27 | 26 | 25 | 24 | 23 | 22 |

To Ambrose Fredstrom Meador,

may you, like your namesakes, always see and love the

wounded and call them to the life of peace.

To the memory of Fr. Teddy Molyneaux,

a faithful priest and courageous Christian. I look forward

to meeting again on the other side of the river.

You who have watched the wings of darkness lifting
and heard the misted whisper of the sea,
shelter your heart with patience now, with patience,
and keep it free.

Let not the voiced destruction and the tumult
urge to a lesser prize your turning mind;
keep faith with beauty now, and in the ending
stars you may find.

JANE TYSON CLEMENT

A theology for our time should help us to know that Being is indeed the
theater of God's glory, and that, within it, we have a terrible privilege,
a capacity for profound error and grave harm. We might venture an
answer to God's question, Where were you when I created—? We were
there, potential and implicit and by the grace of God inevitable, more
unstoppable than the sea, impervious as Leviathan, in that deep
womb of time almost hearing the sons of God when they shouted
for joy. And we are here, your still-forming child, still opening our
eyes on a reality whose astonishments we can never exhaust.

MARILYNNE ROBINSON

Whoever will not be persuaded that he is able to establish a
kingdom of heaven on earth or make out of his own home or
situation a house or temple of God is heading toward the devil.
For where there is service to God, there is heaven. When I serve
my neighbor, I am already in heaven, for I am serving God.

MARTIN LUTHER

CONTENTS

FOREWORD

Karen Swallow Prior

A nswers to the hardest and most complicated questions we face as human beings start to become clearer when we consider telos, or purpose, regarding the components of a given dilemma. Why does this thing exist? What is it for? What is the purpose of this relationship? Of human life? How do we best fulfill our purpose and help others do the same? These questions ought to be asked of forests, railroads, cellphones, and fountain pens as well as of people and communities and institutions. And, as Jake Meador asks in the pages that follow, we ought to ask what Christians are for too.

It is the mark of particularly modern Christians that we have given so much attention to what we do (morality) and what we think (worldview) that we have perhaps forgotten to consider why we are here. It has taken most of my life for me to begin to see what this book reveals so clearly and compellingly—that Christian purpose consists of more than what we do or how we think. Even as someone born into a Christian home and a church-loving family, I became good at compartmentalizing my Christian faith from the rest of life. I didn't even have to try. I was born again but didn't know how to live because I didn't know what my life was for.

I don't think I am alone. For many believers right now, it feels a bit like the end of the world, or at least the end of *a* world. It seems like the church—or at least the twenty-first century American evangelical church—has reached the limits of what right thinking and doing can do for our souls, let alone for the lives we must live together—believer and unbeliever, red state and blue state, urban and rural, healthy and sick, needed and needy—until our lives and this world really do meet their end.

What Are Christians For? Life Together at the End of the World offers moving reminders of times and places in other parts of history that surely felt like the end of the world for those living in them, including those in the church: American slavery, South African apartheid, Nietzsche's existential Europe, and the horrors of the Great War (which would, of course, be followed by even greater horrors decades later).

In fact, it was during this turn-of-the-century context when the Dutch theologian Herman Bavinck developed and articulated his influential idea of the Christian worldview, largely as a response to the insufficient, even false and dangerous, worldviews prevailing in his own age and influencing the church of the time. This history, noted later in this book, reminds us that we who feel out of sorts in the world today are not alone. "The peculiarity of this moment," Bavinck observed of his own moment, as aptly as it could be of our own, "is that everyone feels an epoch of change, when all people realize they cannot remain the same, and that some long for this moment to pass by more swiftly than others. There is a disharmony between our thinking and feeling, between our willing and acting." The words remind us that while the specifics change according to time and circumstance, the calling of Christians remains the same.

This is why the pages that follow in this book are oddly comforting. Jake Meador reminds us that the purpose of the Christian life never changes according to time, place, or station, even if we of particular places and perspectives have difficulty seeing and applying such a complete vision in whole.

Our view is clouded by many things, most of these the consequences of the distortions of modernity. (To be clear, every era has its own deceptions.) Even Christians who believe in and live by the orthodox doctrines of the historic church can't help but be formed also by our larger cultural ethos in which nature is reduced to matter, community is replaced by institutions, the soul is narrowed into a self, and the body becomes merely the sum of its parts. The idols of the world—indeed, the mere idols of modern America—have sometimes, even many times, become idols in the church. We are fools if we fail to recognize that even a Christian worldview based on unchanging eternal truths is not a clouded lens.

What we need, in addition to clearer vision, is a greater sense of wholeness: a whole way of being, one that transcends the distortions of our time.

A revived sense of ourselves as embodied creatures—bodies of particular times and places who are nevertheless like all other human bodies, made in God's image and for a purpose—will help address nearly every crisis we face as a church and a civilization today. We the church are a body, and we each individually are bodies. Christians are a people called to submit to Jesus, both as individuals and as a body, and to others, and to steward the earth he created, and to serve well each body he knitted together. "Persons cannot be whole alone," Wendell Berry observes in *The Unsettling of America*. "If the body is healthy, then it is whole. But how can it be whole and yet be dependent, as it obviously is, upon other bodies and upon the earth, upon all the rest of Creation, in fact? It immediately becomes clear that the health or wholeness of the body is a vast subject, and that to preserve it calls for a vast enterprise."[1]

Yes, it is a vast subject that calls for a vast enterprise. It is vaster than the universe, but not vaster than the Creator and sustainer of that universe. Berry continues, "If the soul is to live in this world only by denying the body, then its relation to worldly life becomes extremely simple and superficial. Too simple and superficial, in fact, to cope in any meaningful or useful way with the world."[2]

Simple and superficial, this book is not. In fact, there is so much wisdom, so much wholeness, in these pages, that to read them is to be left wondering how we have gone so far astray. Indeed, this book fills me with yearning. It sounds a bell that calls all within earshot to come back home and gather around the table for a filling feast that is ours to enjoy forever.

Introduction

WHOLE LIFE POLITICS AT THE END OF THE WORLD

The flight from Johannesburg to London is eighteen hours. It's one of the longest flights in the world. As we boarded the plane, having already made one flight from Lusaka, Zambia, to Jo'burg and now coming off a six-hour layover in the Johannesburg airport, my friends and I were tired, and I didn't pay much attention to the elderly man in a black collared shirt as he sat down next to me.

I struggled to sleep at first and then finally gave up and sat up a little in my seat. Soon the man and I fell into conversation, as people sometimes do on a plane. "What do you do for a living?" I asked him.

"Why don't you guess?" he asked me with a mischievous smile.

"Are you a teacher?" I asked.

"That's part of it."

"A counselor?"

"Oh, yes, certainly that."

"Umm. A lawyer?"

He smiled. "In a manner of speaking."

Finally, I gave up. He smiled again and then reached up to his shirt collar, tucking two fingers into it, and slowly tugged out a white clerical collar, which he had tucked away so as to be less conspicuous, I suppose.

I laughed. He smiled.

"I'm Jake," I said.

"Good to meet you," he replied. "I'm Father Teddy."

A thought occurred to me. This was an elderly, White, Roman Catholic priest living in South Africa in 2007. We were less than twenty years removed from the end of apartheid. Had he been there during the apartheid era, or had he come to the country later? What had he done during those years if he had lived there? I wanted to know, but how do you politely ask that sort of question? I wasn't sure. We continued to make small talk. Eventually he decided to sleep, and I opened up the in-flight movie options and put on my headphones.

I found a 1987 movie I'd not heard of before called *Cry Freedom*, directed by Richard Attenborough. It's the story of Steven Biko, a Black South African activist who was murdered by police while in custody in 1977. Biko was the defining figure in a movement called Black Consciousness that sought to instill a sense of pride, dignity, and self-worth in Black South Africans who had been beaten down by the injustices of apartheid.

Biko's activism had a predictable outcome: He was put under house arrest on specious grounds, arrested when he was caught violating house arrest, and then beaten to death in prison. The government issued a press release claiming he died from a hunger strike. He was thirty years old. Biko left behind a widow and several children and a movement that was yet again without a leader.

The story could have ended there. The South African police killed hundreds, if not thousands, of people during the apartheid era. Biko was not unusual in that respect, even if he was more prominent than many of the other victims. But a friend of Biko's— a White, Catholic journalist named Donald Woods—didn't believe the official account of his death. Biko himself had told Woods that he would never do anything to jeopardize his own health or take his own life if he were imprisoned. He told Woods not to believe it if he died and the government said he had taken his own life. So Woods, using his press credentials, arranged to see Biko's body. He smuggled in a camera, took photos that plainly showed Biko had been beaten to death, and then snuck the film out of the morgue. He sent the photos around the world, telling everyone the truth about what the South African government had done to Steven Biko.

The government responded as you might expect. They put Woods under house arrest. They also began a protracted intimidation campaign that targeted not only Woods but also his wife and children. The police shot bullets into their house at night. They made threatening phone calls. Woods and his wife decided it was time to leave after their five-year-old daughter received a T-shirt in the mail with Biko's face printed on the front that was coated inside with chemicals that burned her face and arms when she tried to put it on.

But how could they escape? Woods was under house arrest. He would need a disguise. He spoke to a friend and they made arrangements. A Catholic priest agreed to give Woods his passport so Woods could disguise himself as a priest and *maybe* slip through the border using the priest's identity. If he was caught, of course, the priest would suffer alongside Woods.

And so one day Woods, his hair dyed black to match the priest's hair and dressed in a black collared shirt and clerical collar, snuck down to his family's garage and lay down on the floor in the backseat of the car as his wife drove out on an errand. Once they'd escaped surveillance, he got out of the car and hitchhiked to the border, where he met the priest, who helped him across. Once he was out of the country, he called his wife, and she and the children followed him across the border. From there they escaped to London, and Woods embarked on a long and storied career of anti-apartheid activism that led to him, at the invitation of President Jimmy Carter, becoming the first private citizen to address the United Nations. It was a remarkable story and a remarkable movie. That night, I fell asleep somewhere over western Africa thinking about Biko and Woods.

When I awoke, we were almost to London. The priest was awake, sipping a cup of coffee. "Forgive me, but I saw the movie you were watching last night," he said. "What did you think of it?" I said I had liked it and asked him if he'd seen it. "Oh yes," he said. "I know it well." I asked him if he remembered Biko—perhaps this was how I could ask the question I had wanted to ask the night before. "Yes, I was in South Africa when Biko was working," he said. "He was a good man. I admired him."

Then he asked me a question: "Did you see the note at the beginning of the film about how two names had been changed in the movie in order to protect certain people?" I remembered it, vaguely. "Well," the priest explained, "they did that because the film was made in 1987. The Afrikaner government was still in power then, and two people involved in that story were still living in South Africa. They would have been in a lot of trouble if their identities had been revealed."

He continued, "One of the two names they changed in the movie was mine."

You can imagine my jaw dropping.

"You were the priest?" I practically shouted on the still mostly sleeping aircraft.

He smiled. "Yes, I gave Donald my passport to use to escape the country. Donald was a good friend and a good man. I miss him." (Woods had died of natural causes several years before I met Fr. Teddy, but he had lived to see the end of apartheid.)

By this time we were beginning our descent. "Tell me everything," I begged. He told me about Biko and Woods and the courage not only of Donald Woods but also of Steve Biko's widow and their children, and of Donald's wife and their children, and of Biko's many friends who carried on his work after he was murdered.

Soon we were at our gate. I found myself wishing that one of the world's longest flights could have been just a little bit longer.

I found the friends I had been with in Zambia by our gate at Heathrow and began telling them about him. "Did you get a picture?" one of them asked. Without answering, I ran off, frantically looking for the priest. Remarkably, I found him. I rushed up to him and asked for a picture. He smiled, and we found someone to take our photo. Then we parted.

To this day, sitting near my desk in my study is a picture of an ordinary Christian man who anonymously did his part to make sure the world knew about the evils being done in South Africa. You have never heard of him, of course, but he is one of whom the world was not worthy, one who has now gone to his reward, having died in 2019 in South Africa among the people he loved and pastored for half a century.

Fr. Ted was not a political radical. Indeed, over the course of his long ministry in South Africa, he kept a remarkably low profile. "He didn't want any police attention," said Dillon Woods, Donald's son, in an interview with Irish radio after Fr. Ted's death.[1] "The police were brutal, killing people left, right, and center." Amidst all this violence and horror, Fr. Ted ministered in rural areas and Black townships, doing the work of an ordinary Catholic priest. He said Mass, he prayed, he gave homilies, he administered last rites, he baptized babies and new converts. He also learned multiple languages, including a clicking dialect that he told me a bit about on the plane, and translated parts of the Bible into the languages of his parishioners. He saw all of this as being part of his calling as a priest.

"It was vital for him not to be getting harassment from the police," said Dillon Woods. "He carried on working in the townships. He raised huge amounts of money for community programs. . . . He thought his calling was his church work, so he didn't want to be in the limelight, so to speak. [His story] only really came out at his funeral [in 2019]." Fr. Ted was a remarkably gifted man, but most of his life was taken up with very ordinary pastoral and missionary work, and that was how he wished it to be. But when he saw a chance to aid a friend in combating social injustice on a larger scale beyond his smaller ministry in the townships, Fr. Ted didn't hesitate. "He was terrified," Dillon Woods said, but even so he did what God called him to do.

Fr. Ted represents a particular approach to Christianity and public life. Most popularly, this approach has been called a "whole life" political philosophy because it is concerned with creating a society that is pervasively open to and supportive of life "from the womb to the tomb," as the saying goes. Such a political system is concerned with both social justice and ordinary Christian piety in the lives of individual believers. It desires to both lift up the poor and protect the unborn. It is, for the most part, a school unrepresented in both contemporary and historical American politics. It is precisely because of this lack that our nation's Christian heritage has always been not merely incomplete but uniquely compromised.

The history of American Christianity is a history of what C. S. Lewis might have called "Christianity and . . ." Lewis developed this idea in *The Screwtape Letters*, where the senior demon instructs an understudy in how to successfully attack the piety and faith of a new believer. If the demon can always keep the "patient's" Christianity intrinsically bound up in something else *in addition* to his Christian faith, then that faith can be made to support virtually anything and will be emptied of much of its transformative power in the life of both the individual person and the broader society. Though there are many variants of "Christianity and," one in particular has long vexed and flayed the body of Christ in America, as well as the American body politic.

The antislavery activist Frederick Douglass was one of the most astute analysts of the ways America's Christian practice has been compromised. Douglass argued that American Christianity has almost always been a kind of accommodated Christianity, modified and adapted to suit the economic desires and personal prejudices of many Americans. The moral claims of Christianity—with the full radicalism not only of the Sermon on the Mount but also, frankly, of the ordinary writings about money, poverty, and neighborly love—were routinely modified and limited in the United States in ways that protected the interests of the wealthy and threatened the basic dignity of Black and Indigenous people.

I will never forget the night I attended a college ministry's Bible study as we read James 1. We came to the famous verse at the end of the chapter, where the author says that pure and undefiled religion in the sight of the Father looks after widows and orphans in their distress. This college ministry was connected to an extremely

wealthy church. Many of us in the room were ourselves comparatively well off. The group leader looked at us and said, "Well, there
are no widows or orphans in our church" (which was not even true),
"so this just means we need to look out for each other." A few
minutes later the study ended, and we went on our way, indifferent
to the fact that there were homeless people sitting on street corners,
hungry and cold, within three blocks of the church-owned house
that hosted the study.

Too often in our nation's history, ordinary believers have been
insulated from the fullness of Christian discipleship; a buffer exists
that separates many spheres of life from the calling of Christ. This
not only affects us but our neighbors as well, who have been too
often deprived of the Christian love we are called to show them. The
result has been a divide between the Christian communal practices
and piety envisioned in much of Scripture and church history on
the one hand and the actual practices and piety of many American
Christians on the other. The problem is an old one, which is why it
is both so pervasive in our day and so difficult to name.

But Frederick Douglass, himself a devout Christian, named it.
Writing in the mid-nineteenth century, he said,

> Between the Christianity of this land, and the Christianity of
> Christ, I recognize the widest possible difference—so wide,
> that to receive the one as good, pure, and holy, is of necessity
> to reject the other as bad, corrupt, and wicked. To be the
> friend of the one, is of necessity to be the enemy of the other.
> I love the pure, peaceable, and impartial Christianity of
> Christ: I therefore hate the corrupt, slaveholding, women-
> whipping, cradle-plundering, partial and hypocritical Christi-
> anity of this land. Indeed, I can see no reason, but the most
> deceitful one, for calling the religion of this land Christianity.
> I look upon it as the climax of all misnomers, the boldest of
> all frauds, and the grossest of all libels.[2]

The Kentucky writer Wendell Berry echoed the concerns of
Douglass over a hundred years later in his book *The Hidden Wound*:

Consider the moral predicament of the master who sat in church with his slaves, thus attesting his belief in the immortality of the souls of the people whose bodies he owned and used. He thus placed his body, if not his mind, at the very crux of the deepest contradiction of his life. How could he presume to own the body of a man whose soul he considered as worthy of salvation as his own? To keep this question from articulating itself in his thoughts and demanding an answer, he had to perfect an empty space in his mind, a silence, between heavenly concerns and earthly concerns, between body and spirit.[3]

It's that space that existed in the minds of White Americans that created our bifurcated, accommodated form of Christianity. The teachings of the Gospels, the Epistles, and the Prophets had to be kept at a distance from the actual realities of life in America. The Dutch Calvinist theologian Herman Bavinck may have summarized the problem most concisely: "If Jesus still wants to retain some authority over us, he has to put up with being injected into the Aryan tribe."[4] Granted, Bavinck was speaking in the European context, but he was addressing a Northern European church that, already in the early 1900s, was showing signs of concern with regard to national idolatry.

Why are the politics of someone like Fr. Ted so uncommon in America? Why is it that in a nation of over three hundred million there are so few prominent representatives of a politics concerned with both righteousness and justice, the life of the family, and the life of the world?

One answer: because too often we have not allowed our would-be Fr. Teds to encounter the full weight and radicalism of the Christian message. The late Michael Spencer lamented this in his final writings, noting that too often the American church shrunk back from Christian discipleship, favoring a path of personal peace and affluence instead of the hard but joyful calling of Christian discipleship. Wealth, comfort, and prejudice have too often conditioned and modified the calling of the Christian religion in America.

This is precisely what happened the night of that college Bible study when we beheld the law of love as given to us in James 1 and our group leader blunted the edge of the command. And the people who suffer because of it are not those who possess the means to be comfortable and secure but those who do not—such as the homeless men sitting on the corner three blocks from where we were piously reading about God's care for the destitute.

The problem is mostly not with ordinary Christian people half-heartedly following Jesus and willfully choosing to ignore certain commandments. The American church is filled with ordinary people who love Jesus and seek to serve him and their neighbors in their daily lives. I have benefited from their kindness and generosity on many occasions. The problem is much more complex than that. It's the way our vision of the Christian life has too often been implicitly conditioned and defined to leave the characteristic idols of the Western world untouched, unscathed, and unchallenged. This is how Christian people, often without even realizing it, are denied access to the life-giving power of Christian piety and discipleship by the very institution that ought to introduce them to it: the church. If our purportedly Christian nation has not produced our own Fr. Teds with more regularity, it is perhaps because we have never actually been a Christian nation.

Certainly, this judgment holds up if we consider the writings of the saints of the past. The sixteenth-century Protestant Reformer Martin Bucer, who mentored a young John Calvin, wrote a great deal about the desirability and goodness of Christian nations, but nearly all of it would seem unsettling and radical to many of today's Christian nationalists. In his book *De Regno Christi*, which he wrote to the English king as instructions for making the English nation more pervasively Christian, Bucer at one point exhorts the king to take seriously the task of aiding the poor: "These practices (to alleviate poverty and assist those in need of work), therefore, which we have mentioned, are proper to the Kingdom of Christ, and all who do not earnestly desire to see them restored, as Christ commanded, openly witness concerning themselves, however they may glory in words about the Kingdom of Christ, that in reality they neither acknowledge it truly nor seek it sincerely."[5] He is saying that those who do not desire to alleviate poverty do not seek God. If you tolerate rampant poverty, then you have no right to call yourself a Christian society. This is jarring for us to read today. And yet Bucer is hardly a fire-breathing radical. He was a mentor to John Calvin and close friend to Philip Melanchthon, Luther's right-hand man in promoting the Lutheran Reformation. In the eyes of many early Reformers, Bucer was both one of the gentlest figures (to a fault, some thought) and one of the most virtuous. If Bucer seems radical to us today, that likely says more about us than it does Bucer.

So what would it mean for America to be an authentically Christian nation? It will mean a repudiation of the beliefs and views that assail the cause of life and threaten justice. It will mean standing for the causes that Fr. Ted stood for. We live in a revolutionary world, a world in which the human person, animals, and even the physical creation itself are reduced to things, made subject to a relentless and cruel force that denies to people and places the "ontological density" that is theirs by right by virtue of being created by God. A whole life Christian politics might be unrecognizable to both Democrats and Republicans alike, but that is only because the dominant political visions of Western life today are so deeply inhumane and deeply anti-Christian. But it doesn't have to be this way. Through their fidelity to both righteousness and justice, ordinary Christians like Fr. Ted show us a still better way.

1

AN IMMENSE INHERITANCE

A Christian Account of Nature

When you're a college student, you never want to find yourself in a position that requires a late-night call home for help. Unfortunately, on New Year's Eve 2009, I found myself in such a situation. I had stopped by a New Year's Eve party for a short time that evening but left early without talking to many people or even having a drink. I spent a bit of time at home by myself—my roommates were all at the party—before deciding to get in my car and drive out into the country.

I would be graduating in five months. Then two days after graduation I was planning to move six hours away from the only home I'd ever known—Lincoln, Nebraska—to St. Paul, Minnesota. I had a lot on my mind and needed the stillness of the country. One benefit of living in Lincoln is that you're never more than twenty or thirty minutes away from gravel country roads and the silence and starlight they can offer after dark. So I bundled up, got in my car, and drove out into the dark and cold of the Nebraska winter night. It was two degrees Fahrenheit when I left home.

I got about twenty miles southwest of town and decided to pull onto the shoulder of the road and get out to walk a bit. I hadn't seen a car for some time and figured I'd be safe if I stayed far enough to the side of the road. I rang in the New Year smoking my pipe and looking at the stars. There is a quiet about rural Nebraska that I find captivating.

There is something uniquely beautiful about cold winter nights. The snow seems to absorb sounds, lending a quiet to the place that exceeds even what is normal for rural America. What you are left with is silence and the immensity of the sky, stretching out into infinity across the farmland, while stray plants poke up through the white, and the occasional tree, branches heavy with snow, reaches upward in a muted gesture of praise to its maker. It's cold and ominous, yet somehow still feels homelike.

There's just enough life cracking through the snow and reaching skywards to know that these are not unending snows, but rather an interim, even a necessary part of the life of the place. The snowmelt will help nourish the ground and prepare it for planting come spring. Even in winter there is life to be seen if you know where to look and how to listen. What looks "dead" to many people is actually thrumming with life.

Such knowledge changes how you look at the place. When you look up to the stars you do not see a sterilized "space," a blank expanse of cold deadness. You see the heavens, the fields of the gods, peopled by more stars than you'll ever see in the city.

On that night I needed to feel small and yet still at home in the world. To be alive and yet to know oneself to be only a portion of something similarly alive and yet much greater is a comfort. "The world is charged with the grandeur of God," wrote Gerard Manley Hopkins.[1] I can think of few ways to be better reminded of that than to walk on gravel country roads late at night, hearing the crunch of snow beneath your feet as you stare at the stars above, almost imagining that they are, as many who came before us believed, living beings looking down on you.

Then I turned to walk back to my car. And as I approached it, my attention was roughly drawn back to more banal matters, like "being able to get home." Had I really pulled *that* far onto the shoulder? I approached the passenger side of the car and noticed both passenger-side tires had sunk alarmingly deep into the snow. Swallowing slowly, I got into my car, turned it on, and tried to steer back onto the road. Instead of pulling onto the road, I heard the dreaded sound that many Midwesterners know well: wheels spinning futilely in the snow.

I got out, used a snow shovel I had in the trunk (a gift from my parents, who know me well) and tried to scoop some of the snow away. It didn't work. I then tried calling my roommates—no answer. And so I found myself stuck on the side of Denton Road, twenty miles southwest of Lincoln in zero-degree weather a little after midnight on New Year's Day 2010. I had two choices.

First, I could sit in my car and hope my hat, heavy wool coat, gloves, wool socks, and boots could keep me warm till morning, when I could call my roommates to come dig me out. (When would they be up anyway?)

Second, I could call my parents. (There are many benefits to living in one's hometown.)

I called my parents.

Mom groggily answered, her voice immediately becoming sharper and more alert when she realized who was calling and what time he was calling at. I assured her I was okay and then asked if I could talk to Dad. She passed the phone, and I explained my situation to him. "Stay there," he said. "I'm on my way." So Dad got out of bed, got dressed, and drove out to meet me, arriving about forty-five minutes later.

When he got there, he looked around and under my car, and then he looked briefly at me. He didn't say much. Without a word or even a shake of his head, he shoveled a bit more of the snow away. Then he told me to start the car. He said to put it in the lowest gear and slowly depress the gas pedal. He opened the passenger door, stood just inside the open door without getting in the car, and braced his shoulder against the frame of the vehicle. Then he pushed. As he pushed, he coached me on how to steer the car out. Slowly, we got the car onto the road.

I thanked him, then I apologized for probably the third or fourth time. He said it was okay. He asked if I knew how to get back into town.

"Yeah, I can manage that," I told him.

He looked at me for a moment and then said, "Why don't you follow me anyway."

It wasn't a question.

Chastened, I followed him back into town. As we reached the western edge of the city, he turned into a gas station. I turned in after him and we both got out of our cars. By now it was nearly two in the morning. The temperature was well below zero.

"Don't do that again," he said.

"I won't," I said. "Thanks."

Dad laughed for the first time since he arrived on the scene.

"I had an old truck when I was your age. You should've seen the ways I got it stuck. My dad always came to get me." Then he said good night, got in his car, and drove home.

I arrived at my duplex a few minutes later and saw, somewhat to my relief, that my roommates were still out. I went to bed.

AGAINST DEBT-FREE LIVING

Behind that simple story of a father going out into the dark and cold to rescue his child is a profound truth, at least if you understand the story as my dad did. Responding to this situation was not difficult for him, at least in one sense. There was no question for him of what he needed to do as soon as he heard about my situation. He needed to go out there and find me and get me out of the ditch and get me safely home. There could be no other choice. It was simply the "right" thing to do. How did he know this? Well, there are many ways that he knew it, but the reason he gave that night when we were standing out in the cold was simple: his dad did the same thing for him. One generation's patient kindness and care for the next creates a sort of debt, but unlike the financialized forms of debt that most of us know so well today, this is good debt.

The idea of good debt might sound strange. We are mostly familiar these days with student loan debt, or credit card debt, or perhaps the exorbitant and unjust debt foisted on the poor by payday loan companies. Even the debts that help us accrue wealth, such as mortgages, can create an enormous amount of stress and anxiety. This is, perhaps, why so many people have become preoccupied with "debt-free living." Whether from the financial gurus on the right who advise people how to get out of debt on their own, or from the economic populists of the left who seek federal-level solutions to the problem of consumer debt, the normative assumption across much of the United States today is that debt is bad and living free of debt is good.

What this ignores, however, is that living completely free of debt is to live completely free of relationships, or at least to live free of formalized relationships that have defined expectations of what is given and received between the two parties. To live without debt is to live without dependencies, and dependencies are a central part of the good life. Indeed, living in relationships of mutual dependence is something humans do naturally. Consider the complex web of interdependencies that shape a family. Such dependent relationships can, like all things, be twisted and perverted, as is the case with financialized debt in the United States. The solution to this problem is not to eradicate dependence but to establish better grounds for our relationships and to recognize how relationships of care are a necessary part of providing for the weak and how every single one of us will, at many points in our life, be weak.

The Swiss Reformed theologian Emil Brunner said that each of us receives an "immense inheritance" at our birth.[2] Inheritances, of course, are beneficent gifts passed on to us by those who came before. They are graces we receive through no merit of our own. For Brunner and for Christianity, in fact, the world is a gift; indeed, existence is a gift. It is not without its pain because we live in the aftermath of the cosmic disaster that was humanity's fall into sin. But even so, there remain vestiges of nobility in humanity and vestiges of beauty in the world. And so each of us enters the world being owed certain things and, eventually, owing things to others. The newborn baby is owed care and attention by his or her parents. The business owner owes a just wage to his employees. Husbands owe love, honor, and fidelity to their wives. Parents owe the fruit of their work to their children. The government owes physical safety and security to its citizens. This is justice, of course; justice is merely giving to a person what they are owed. When we speak of justice, we are inextricably speaking in terms of inheritances and obligations.

A healthy society recognizes these truths and hardwires them into its life through a variety of means—laws, certainly, but also customs, traditions, and rituals that all help undergird and solidify the relationships of mutuality and care that allow for human flourishing. It is to our great detriment and loss that we do not live in a society that recognizes these truths. If we are to return to flourishing, health, and life, then we will need to figure out how the inheritance was lost and how we came to forget that we exist in natural webs of affection, care, and obligation.

To understand how this was lost, we need to consider the historical story we find ourselves in more closely and examine the key turns in our thought that have led us to our current state in which our society is increasingly cold, cruel, and heartless. How did a people who once understood and passed on the "immense inheritance" come to trade all that in for what Pope John Paul II has called "the culture of death"?[3]

ORPHANS IN THE COSMOS

In one sense, of course, it is not hard to understand how so many people came to this view. Even if we limit ourselves to considering the past hundred years of human history, we find ourselves facing two horrible world wars, the Russian Revolution, the Holocaust, the American firebombing campaigns in Europe and Japan, and the advent of the atom bomb, to say nothing of a host of lesser-known atrocities. It is not difficult to understand how someone could look at all that, judge the earth to be an unimaginable cavalcade of cruelty and calamity, and imagine an escape from it as being their best hope for salvation.

Theologian Paul Griffiths speaks truly when he says that "the nonhuman animate world is an ocean of blood flowing from violent death; and the human world differs from it in this only in the scale of the violence and the ingenuity of its performance, in both of which our world far exceeds the nonhuman one. . . . We are born into a damaged world, and we then proceed to damage both it and ourselves further."[4]

Our world can often seem like a cold, indifferent machine whose chief output is misery and mayhem. Talk of an "immense inheritance" by contrast can seem remote or perhaps even an insult that ignores or trivializes the presence of suffering, evil, and pain.

The German sociologist Hartmut Rosa summarizes this experience of the world by saying that under modernity, particularly late modernity, you and I encounter the world as "a point of aggression."[5] And, of course, if the world is chiefly a point of aggression, then the only thing for people to do is either to escape it or, failing that, to acquire power and assert their control over it.

The struggles that define our day, then, are not new. These difficult questions—concerning questions of public justice; or the human person, sexuality, and gender; or the myriad issues related to climate change—are all predictable questions that will arise when our primary experience of the world is one of suffering and alienation, when the world feels to us like it is chiefly a point of aggression.

A PLAN OF LOVE AND TRUTH

Despite all this, I think we are still on good ground when we view the world as our immense inheritance, as a gift rather than a prison to be escaped. The Dutch Calvinist Herman Bavinck, who lived and wrote in the late nineteenth and early twentieth centuries, can be a helpful guide in answering that question. Bavinck was concerned by a felt dissonance in the soul that seemed to pervade the Europe of his day, a dissonance that will sound familiar to us today: "The peculiarity of this moment is that everyone feels an epoch of change, when all people realize they cannot remain the same, and that some long for this moment to pass by more swiftly than others. There is a disharmony between our thinking and feeling, between our willing and acting. There is a discord between religion and culture, between science and life."[6]

Bavinck believed that the dominant spirit behind all these questions and social transformations was that of the German philosopher Friedrich Nietzsche. Nietzsche, Bavinck argued, recognized that if Europe really had moved beyond Christianity, then everything would need to change because virtually everything about European culture, politics, and even practical day-to-day life was shaped in some measure by Christianity. If Christianity were to be rejected, everything else would need to be "reset," one might say. Value systems, human communities, national politics—everything— would need to be redefined and reevaluated in the aftermath of the failure of Christianity and the ascent of late modernity. Ultimately, Nietzsche called for the rise of the Übermensch, or the "over man," who "prefers the concreteness of domination to the flighty pursuit of happiness."[7] If the world is a point of aggression, then one way of dealing with that is to rise above the world in power and might.

Bavinck saw his task in *The Christian Worldview* to be offering his readers an alternative to the Nietzschean account of the world—to recatechize Christian people, as it were, and to help them once again find in Christianity a plausible and life-affirming account of reality. He did this in a way that might surprise contemporary readers. He did not begin by attempting a propositional defense of certain core Christian doctrines, nor did he provide an overview of the Christian story of creation, fall, redemption, and restoration. Instead, Bavinck took up several classic philosophical problems, devoting one chapter to each, and tried to demonstrate two things: First, the Nietzschean account of these questions, "What am I?" and "What is the world?" and "What is my place and task in the world?" are unsatisfying because they are too simplistic. Second, the Christian account is more satisfying because it is able to affirm reality in its complexity, rather than subduing reality to its ideological aspirations, like a philosopher trying to cram the square peg of reality into the round hole of his particular philosophy.

In particular, Bavinck was concerned with distinguishing between the "organic" element in the Christian worldview and the "mechanical" elements he saw as being inextricably bound up with the Nietzschean framework. It may be helpful to consider a specific example to help make the difference between the two a bit clearer: What does the Nietzschean mean when he talks about "nature"? And what, in contrast, does a Christian mean when talking about "nature"?

In the mechanical view of the world, Bavinck says, the universe is impersonal and indifferent to you and me. It is simply a sort of grand, cosmic machine, complicated to be sure, but ultimately predictable and devoid of any sort of ultimate goal or end. The universe isn't bending toward any final destination. It simply is. So when the mechanistic person talks about nature, they mean a kind of order that is governed by these unbreakable physical laws that govern how the machine operates—gravity, entropy, and so on. Nature is governed by these laws, which are indifferent to morality or right or wrong. Thus nature has no moral content to it and so is finally "red in tooth and claw," as Tennyson once put it.[8]

But this explanation is not altogether satisfactory. There is something beautiful in the natural world, and we encounter it nearly every day—the delightful song of birds singing in a tree, the smell of fresh flowers growing outside one's front door, the amusing play of two squirrels chasing each other in the park. While the things that cause Tennyson to speak of nature in such brutal ways are true, they are not the whole truth of the natural world. Indeed, there is a genius in much of nature that supersedes that of humanity, as our climate crisis exposes for all to see. There is violence in the world to be sure, and it sometimes appears to be governed by an indifferent cruelty. But that is not the whole truth about nature.

Bavinck recognizes this:

> Nature is no foolish, brutal, or demonic power but a means to the revelation of God's thoughts and virtues. Nature is an unfurling of his wisdom and a reflection of his glory. In defiance of all disharmony between virtue and happiness, the

world is still a suitable place for the human being to live—not heaven, but also not hell, not paradise but also not a wasteland, a domicile that corresponds with his present condition. Under the influence of Darwinism, the thought has emerged that this world was nothing other than a scene of struggle and misery. But this representation is as equally one-sided as is the idyllic-nature view of the eighteenth century. Scripture avoids both extremes; it rejects the optimism and the pessimism in their falsehood but after having first fully recognized the elements of truth that are hidden in both.[9]

What Bavinck wanted to preserve was an account of the natural world that recognized that nature was more than mere matter and that nature was made with some future end or goal in mind. And even as nature itself groans beneath the weight of human sin, and even as human beings struggle to perceive nature's beauty and final end because we too are afflicted by sin, still these things remain true. The world as it exists today is not our final home because it is still the aftermath of a violent cosmic cataclysm. But it is also a coherent natural order even now, and we belong to it as creatures made within it. Thus we should not worship nature, but neither should we seek to escape it.

In preserving this more complex account of nature, Bavinck is simply standing in the broad Christian tradition. The same view of nature has been presented more recently by Pope Benedict XVI, who has said that "what we call 'nature' in a cosmic sense has its origin in 'a plan of love and truth.'"[10] And so, Bavinck argued, we can reckon with the real evil in the world while still recognizing that the world is best received by us as a gift, an inheritance left to us by our predecessors and, ultimately, by God himself. It may not be perfect, but even today it is a fit home for us.

CAN WE PERCEIVE NATURE TRULY?

This raises a second problem, however. Let's grant that Bavinck is right. Nature possesses a certain order within itself; it even has a moral trajectory that culminates in the restoration of nature to its full and final glory by God. Participating in this order is how we experience the good life and pass on the good life to the next generation.

But how accessible to us *is* that natural order today? Can we look at reality as we experience it every day and, using our reason, say true things about it? Can nature, rightly understood, guide and shape us? Or is that natural order, to the extent that it still exists in our damaged world, totally inaccessible to us because of sin? And if it is inaccessible to us, how do we find our bearings in the world and know who we are and what we ought to do?

This was not a trivial question, particularly in the decades following Bavinck's death in 1921. The foremost critic of the idea that we could come to true knowledge of the world simply via our reason was the great Swiss Reformed theologian Karl Barth. The Dutch-American theologian Cornelius Van Til arrived at a similar conclusion regarding nature in the US context. If Nietzsche imagined a bombed-out world of gray, dusty chaos waiting to be subdued by the *Übermensch*, Barth and Van Til held that, whatever the world might be, we stagger about in it like those who are blind unless we avail ourselves of the Word of God, which alone can help us see the world truly. Barth came by this view honestly. He feared that appeals to nature inevitably collapsed into a purely arbitrary attempt to legitimize one's personal beliefs and biases. At its worst, Barth warned, this sort of "natural theology" could be used to justify great evils, as he saw happening in Nazi Germany at the time.

In Barth's view, if we say that anything other than the Word of God revealed through Jesus is revelation from God, then we will end up elevating the arbitrary opinions of people to the status of divine revelation. Once you have done that, you can justify virtually anything—even a holocaust. This is why, in the mid-1930s, Barth issued an angry denunciation of "natural theology" as taught by Brunner in a tract titled simply *Nein!*, which is German for "No!" The only revelation humankind receives from God, Barth insisted, is the revelation of God in Christ. Any other source of knowledge is questionable and uncertain and must be kept firmly subservient to the Word of God.

There are other reasons to sympathize with Barth besides his own experience with the German church's capitulation to Nazism. If you have spent much time around certain conservative evangelical circles, you have likely seen certain gender roles that developed in the postwar era of the 1950s discussed as if they are the "natural" way of relating for men and women. So too appeals to nature often undergirded much racial injustice in the nineteenth and early twentieth centuries. Appeals to nature can be abused in precisely the way Barth feared.

Yet the argument against natural theology is not as airtight as some might think. C. S. Lewis observed the same events that drove Barth to reject natural theology but arrived at opposite conclusions. He begins his case for Christianity in *Mere Christianity* with an observation that nearly every day we hear people of all sorts speaking to one another in terms that suggest they share common moral commitments. If a boy at school complains that he shared his candy with a friend yesterday, but the friend is not returning the favor today, he is appealing to a moral standard that he thinks both he and his friend are subject to. Likewise, today when economic populists complain about growing discrepancies between CEO pay and worker pay, they're appealing to a certain standard of fairness they think should apply to worker and CEO alike.

This simple belief is more significant than it might first appear. What this means is that, in at least this one area, people are able, simply on the basis of reason, to recognize a commonly shared reality that both of them are subject to. These somewhat intuitive norms regarding fairness, justice, and so on suggest that it is still, even after the advent of sin, possible to arrive at truth through our reason. It is not a perfect process, nor is it immune to error. But it is *possible*.

Indeed, Lewis recognized something else in making his appeal against both Nietzsche and Barth. If we do not share any common facts or common reality with our neighbors, if we are all inextricably locked up in our own prejudices and follies and can only arrive at truth through the Word of God, then there is actually no basis for life together among those who do not confess the Christian faith. The possibility of persuasion and a healthy pluralism is intrinsically dependent on the idea that two neighbors can access the same reality together through observation and careful thought, and then reason about it together. If there is no shared reality, there is no basis for shared reasoning. Ironically, the Barthian turn against reason actually leaves us in the same place as the Nietzschean revolution that Bavinck opposed: There is no natural order that you and I exist within and must share; there is only our competing wills. In such a state, the only way of avoiding conflict is for each of us to make what some have called the "retreat to commitment."

The retreat to commitment happens when a person says that they have committed themselves to a certain identity, belief system, or community, and their commitment to it is, in itself, what keeps them there. In Christian theology this has sometimes been called "fideism." But a similar logic can be seen outside the church today, as when a person simply declares that "whatever a person thinks they are, that's what they are." That person's commitment to their identity is, therefore, immune to any claims that might be made through moral reasoning.

The difficulty here is that such an argument is immune to any sort of real critique because it is grounded entirely in human choice. There is no basis for distinguishing between choices and no way for people committed to one belief or community to communicate meaningfully with those who have made other commitments. All reasoning, all exchanging of ideas and seeking after grounds for a common, pluralistic life together, is lost in the haze of a reasonless human choice.

This, then, is why we need a firm commitment to the idea that there is such a thing as a natural order that can be observed and understood. Apart from it, we will be condemned to the very thing we are now experiencing in the Western world: cloistered-off communities unable to talk to one another or even to understand one another, for they have nothing in common about which to talk. Bavinck's appeal to nuance and complexity was not simply an academic being pedantic; it was a serious recognition that apart from such things it will be very difficult to form and maintain authentic community.

WHAT IF THE INHERITANCE ISN'T PASSED ON?

Suppose it is true that we are not, in fact, cosmic orphans but rather the recipients of a great inheritance. And suppose that we can discern what that inheritance is and how we ought to pass it on to others. Even granting all of that, one obvious problem remains: we human beings constantly fail to honor the debts we owe to one another. The greatest problem for the idea that nature is the product of "a plan of love and truth" is not necessarily the sophisticated arguments of nineteenth-century philosophers or twentieth-century theologians. It is, rather, the plain fact that the debts we owe to one another are constantly defaulted on—that we constantly fail one another. In a world of such constant failures, it makes a certain sense to say, "I will take control of my life and take care of myself." If no one else will do it, you are all that you have left, or so the common wisdom goes.

It is true that families can fail to practice love. It is true that neighborhoods can be treacherous and friends can fail. And all these failures make it harder to discern, let alone embrace, the natural order that God imprinted on the world when he made it. Yet these failures are not the end of our indebtedness or the destruction of the natural order. Why is that? Answering the question will require a bit of theology, but being able to answer this objection is vital, and so the effort to think through the question carefully will be well rewarded.

Christianity has traditionally taught that God is *simple*. When we use that word conversationally, we mean something like "the opposite of complex." But that is not what simplicity means when Christians are talking about God. When Christians say that God is simple, they mean he does not have multiple parts. He is one. Christianity teaches that when we talk about God, we cannot distinguish between God's being—the blunt fact of his existence—and God's characteristics—his love, his mercy, his justice, and all the rest.

This can seem an abstract debate at first. Why do Christians care about this? What difference does it make whether God has separate parts to his identity? But the answer is quite practical. Classical Christian theism has said that there is nothing that can act on God from the outside, for there is nothing that exists independent of God that can sustain its existence without God. So we cannot think of God's love and God's holiness as being competing characteristics within his being, as if God confronts something happening in the world and has to decide how to respond by balancing his love for people with his regard for his own holiness. That is not how Christianity has understood God traditionally. If that were how we thought of God, we would implicitly be saying that something outside of God is influencing him, either nudging him to favor his love or to favor his holiness. Once we have done that, we have functionally reduced God to a kind of superpowered human, something closer to the Greek gods than to the Christian God. This we should not do—for if you know your Greek mythology, you know that the humanized gods of the Greek myths are often vindictive, petty, and cruel. But God is none of those things.

Rather, because his being and his attributes are the same, we can say that God is complete in himself. The needs and lacks that drive the Greek gods toward vicious behavior simply do not apply to God as he is described in Christianity. Alone among all the beings in existence, God needs nothing outside of himself to sustain his existence or to give him pleasure. He has no need within himself. This can, wrongly understood, cause God to seem aloof and distant. Yet this is precisely the opposite of what our conclusion ought to be from this teaching.

God is complete in himself. He does not need anything else to be satisfied. And yet you and I still exist. This world still exists. The flowers are dressed in splendor, the birds sing with joy, the ocean roars in praise of God. If God is complete in himself and lacks nothing, and if God still moved to create, then he did not create out of some need or fear or insecurity. God did not act because he desires power or wishes to control people or cause them pain. He already is fully powerful, fully realized, fully satisfied within his own inner life. He did not create because he had to. He created because he loves. Creation is gratuitous. It is unnecessary. It is a gift. God in his action is utterly free from all the things that drive human creatures to act sinfully toward their neighbors. And in that there is great comfort because we know when he acts *toward* us, he acts *for* us, for he has no need of anything from us.

Our existence itself is a gift of God. Indeed, the entire cosmos is a gift of God. It is the product of divine intentionality, a means through which God can give of himself to us. Thus even if the more immediate ways in which the world can reveal its order to you—such as family or church or neighborhood—have failed you, that order can still be seen because you have been given the gift of existence by God. The late English theologian John Webster explains it well: "Because God is not one being and agent alongside others, and because he is in himself entirely realized and possesses perfect bliss, he has nothing to gain from creating. Precisely in the absence of divine self-interest, the creature gains everything."[11] Elsewhere in that same essay, Webster quotes the nineteenth-century German Lutheran Isaak Dorner who said, "Love is also a lover of life." And in that, there is some comfort—and even joy.

It is precisely because God exists outside of us that we can receive his law as good. It is because God, acting in love, made the world that we can be confident that the world is good, that the way in which God made the world to work is good. In one of his sermons, Webster writes that "God's law is not an arbitrary set of statutes managed by some divine magistrate; still less is it a mechanism for relating to God through a system of rewards for good conduct and punishments for misbehavior. God's law is best thought of as God's personal presence. It is God's gift of himself, in which he comes to his people in fellowship and sets before them his will for human life. God's law is the claim that God makes upon us as our Maker and Redeemer."[12]

God looks at this world and loves it, which is why we can and should do the same. This world is not something we should seek to escape through conquest or bend to our will through technique, power, or control. Rather, it is a gift given to us by God for our joy and his glory. Because God is love and his law is good, we can look at our neighbor and love him or her. Because God gave himself to us, we can give ourselves to others. We can confidently and joyfully enter into these debts of love that we build up over a lifetime of living in the world, and we can dispense them with extravagance, trusting that whatever wrongs we might experience today as a result of such living will be gathered up and made right in the glorious and perfect love of God.

2

THE GREAT UPROOTING

Race and the End of Nature

The great twentieth-century philosopher Hannah Arendt opens her book *The Human Condition* by observing that the climax of the modern age came in the fall of 1957. On October 4, Soviet scientists successfully launched a small probe the size of a beach ball into orbit. It circled the earth 1,440 times over the next three months before it burned up on reentry into the Earth's atmosphere in January 1958.

This occasion, Arendt said, was the completion of the modern project. Why was that? Because, she said, the modern project began with man rejecting his Father, God, and now it climaxed with the escape from his mother, the Earth. To be truly free, man had to leave both father and mother behind. Until he did that, he would remain a child. With the advent of the space race, humanity finally came to maturity.

This is precisely how the space race was perceived by many on both sides of the Iron Curtain. One American journalist wrote that the launching of Sputnik represented humanity's first "step toward escape from men's imprisonment to the earth." Likewise, the inscription on a Russian scientist's grave, tellingly shaped, like the Tower of Babel, as an obelisk stretching into the sky, read, "Mankind will not remain bound to the earth forever."[1] Sputnik declared that orphaned humanity had come into its own. The world of Sputnik is a world that rejects Brunner's inheritance because it has come to regard the inheritance as being a fiction, at best, and a gross abuse at worst. We have already sketched out a picture of how Christianity imagines the natural world. But now we must tell, in a condensed form, the story Arendt was preoccupied with as she began her study of human society and work, which is the story of modernity—the story of how humanity turned away from both Father and mother and thus became orphaned in the cosmos.

In a 1930 letter written to his friend Arthur Greeves, C. S. Lewis reflected on the ways he and his friends had come to a very different relationship to their place than their ancestors had to their own. Citing his friend J. R. R. Tolkien, Lewis wrote,

> Tolkien once remarked to me that the feeling about home must have been quite different in the days when a family had fed on the produce of the same few miles of country for six generations, and that perhaps this was why they saw nymphs in the fountains and dryads in the woods—they were not mistaken for there was in a sense a real (not metaphorical) connection between them and the countryside. What had been earth and air & later corn, and later still bread, really was in them. We of course who live on a standardized international diet . . . are really artificial beings and have no connection (save in sentiment) with any place on earth. We are synthetic men, uprooted. The strength of the hills is not ours.[2]

This attachment to specific lands, animals, crops, and so on is a central concern for both Lewis and Tolkien. Tolkien's stories are overflowing with people who have the sort of bond with their place that he described in that conversation with Lewis. The Hobbits have been in the Shire for centuries. But still older and stronger are the bonds that tie the Elves to their various homes or the people of Gondor to theirs. Even a comparatively young people, like the people of Rohan, are described as having a language that sounds like the land they live on—sometimes rolling and musical, sometimes harsh and rough as mountains.

Or consider the attachment many of Lewis's characters form to Narnia in his much-loved children's series. There's a sense of being bonded to particular places in characters like Caspian and Tirian, to say nothing of the Pevensie children.

What both Lewis and Tolkien are describing is a thick sense of identity, a sense that goes beyond the space of our own bodies and encompasses our surroundings: our neighbors, the landscape, the plants and trees, the animals—the whole life of the place. For Lewis and Tolkien, all of this is part of what makes you you.

There are others who endorse this view as well. Emil Brunner says that being human means "existence in responsibility."[3] He suggests the image of a suspension bridge as a fitting way of imagining human identity. Suspension bridges are held up by supports on both sides. Brunner suggests that these supports are, on the one side, our sense of self (our desires, ambitions, likes and dislikes, and so on), and on the other side, our sense of place (our neighbors, culture, and so on). Our true identity hangs in the middle, upheld by both of these supports. Likewise, the Spanish philosopher Julian Marias says that the proper way of identifying and understanding ourselves is to say "I am myself *and* my circumstances."[4]

Perhaps the most jarring and robust statement of this idea comes from the Dutch theologian Herman Bavinck, whose doctrine of creation we would do well to recover:

> Nature, as regarded in the Christian religion, is thus much more capacious and richer than the concept that dominates current-day natural science. . . . *Nature* encompassed the entirety of the creation, the spiritual as well as the material. Sometimes the concept was expanded even further and also applied to the Creator. God was "the self-causing activity of nature," the "sum of nature," and all being, the invisible as well as the visible, the creating as well as the created, was summarized together under the one name of *nature*.[5]

This way of framing the issue is even more striking than that of Lewis and Tolkien, Brunner, or Marias because Bavinck goes so far as to suggest that in understanding our relationship to the "natural" world, human beings must not only imagine their relationship to plants and animals and neighbors but even to God himself. The web of life thus becomes immeasurably denser.

The human person does not exist alone in the world, detached and autonomous. Rather, we all exist within nature, which means that we live in tight relationships with the world, our neighbors, and God. The mature person understands how to thrive within such complex relationships and is able to ensure that these relationships are defined by care, love, and the submission of our selfish desires and needs to the law of the natural world. For these Christian thinkers, it is in this state of contingency and interdependence that we find our true selves.

Place is an important word here. When we speak of "places" in this way, we are, to borrow a phrase from Yale theologian Willie Jennings, talking about something that is "ontologically dense," meaning that these places are heavy with life, even overflowing. The good life for human beings is the life that exists in concert with the life of the world. Tolkien's creation myth, the Ainulindalë, offers a striking picture of this. He imagines the creation of the world as a song, slowly built and performed first by the Creator God and then by all his creatures. The blessed life is thus quite literally singing the song the gods have already begun to sing—adding our voices to it and discovering new harmonies and minor themes in their great music.

What Lewis and Tolkien recognized is that the natural world is an essential part of our experience of belonging, of being at home in the world. Tolkien seems to suggest that if we have become disenchanted under modernity, it isn't because anything has changed in people but because we have grown distant from the land, from our home places. It turns out that there's a close tie between enchantment and familiarity.

In trying to reckon with the scale of our estrangement from one another and from the very idea of "home," we should start with understanding our estrangement from nature. There was a time when Christians praised God and thanked him for "Brother Sun" and "Sister Moon," for "Brothers Wind and Air" and "Sister Water," and even for "Mother Earth." Those are the words that the medieval saint Francis of Assisi used in his "Canticle of All Creatures." But today we have grown far from these siblings. And that alienation from our siblings in nature has led to our estrangement from our human siblings as well.

THE LOSS OF PLACE

How did this estrangement come about? There are many answers to this, but since we are considering the natural world here, we should begin by asking how this happened *materially*. What factors that shape our material experience of the world caused us to no longer see "Sister Water" or "Mother Earth," and instead to see raw materials to be used, exploited, and extracted? What material shifts in the world caused us to see our human neighbors in the same way—as naked resources to be consumed as we have need, but not to be loved or attended to as God's beloved creation? Jennings suggests that the answer to this question requires us to reach back to the dawn of the modern age and the turns of thought that developed in response to the conquering of the Americas in the sixteenth century.

In 1572 a Spanish Jesuit theologian named José Acosta sailed from his native Spain for what is now South America. His eventual destination was Peru, where he was to begin work as a theology professor at a university recently established by the Spanish colonizers. He would do the work the Jesuits had become known for: bringing the Christian faith (as understood by the Roman Catholic Church) to parts of the world where it had been forgotten or never been heard before.

As he sailed, Acosta crossed the equator and entered the Southern Hemisphere. This was still a fearful thing for many—a number of Europeans believed the southern seas to be boiling hot and filled with wild, dangerous monsters. If the heat didn't get you, the exotic creatures would. But when Acosta crossed into the southern seasons, nothing happened. The Southern Hemisphere was radically different from how European scientists and theologians had imagined it. He wrote,

> As I had read the exaggerations of the philosophers and poets, I was convinced that when I reached the equator I would not be able to bear the dreadful heat; but the reality was so different that at the very time I was tossing it I felt such cold that at times I went out into the sun to keep warm, and it was the time of year when the sun is directly overhead, which is in the sign of Aries, in March. I will confess here that I laughed and jeered at Aristotle's meteorological theories and his philosophy, seeing that in the very place where, according to his rules, everything must be burning and on fire, I and all my companions were cold.[6]

This may seem like a banal observation to us today, accustomed as we are to traveling distances that would have been unthinkable to Acosta and his peers. But the shift that happens in Acosta in this moment is significant—and it is reflective of a broader change that begins to take root in European Christianity from this time. They had found a new world. The certainties and assumptions of the old had been thrown into doubt. What would replace them? They were confronted by the question that nearly all of us have had to face at some point in our lives, a question that is central to Jennings's work: "Who am I in this strange new place?"[7]

It's a good question. But unfortunately the answer that Acosta and others came to was not only wrong but deeply dangerous. Their answer would pave the way for the events and beliefs that caused us to lose the immense inheritance. The understanding and experience of the world shared among the peoples of North America was in many ways similar to the understanding of Lewis and Tolkien as well as St. Francis. In my own state of Nebraska, one of the main Native American nations was the Omaha people, for whom our state's largest city is named. The Omaha once lived across much of my home state's lands, as well as parts of western Iowa and South Dakota. Today they are confined to a small reservation in the northeastern corner of Nebraska. When their nation stretched across the Great Plains, the Omaha would speak of the "Buffalo Nation" in the same way they might speak of the Sioux Nation. They recognized that the buffalo were not simply a commodity but rather their neighbors and a necessary part of the life of their shared home. Here we can see Brunner's suspension bridge in action, as the push-pull of rooted life in a place helps to shape and guide how people relate to the land, the animals, and one another.

Tragically, this understanding was assailed relentlessly by the colonialists until it was almost entirely eradicated. What replaced this older vision of life? Jennings describes it this way: "Acosta thus fashioned a theological vision for the New World that drew its life from Christian orthodoxy and its power from conquest."[8] What did "conquest" mean in this case? In one sense, the meaning is clear: the theft of land and seizure of resources.

But there's a deeper logic to the idea of conquest that we need to understand. What happens in the conquest of the Americas is a betrayal of the closeness that ought to exist between people and place; the colonialists, whose identity in Europe was closely tied to land, family, and so on, did not seek to inform their identity in this new place in the same way. Instead, they "self-designated," as Jennings puts it. They chose for themselves what their identity would be, independent of any encounter with this new place they had entered. As a result, the dense web of life found in the Americas was diminished in their eyes, reduced to mere matter. Consider the way that Pedro de León, one of the early explorers of the Americas, describes his encounter with the Inca peoples in the Andes of modern-day Peru: "And that God could have permitted something so great would be hidden from the world for so many years and such a long time, and not known by men, yet that it would be found and discovered and won, all in the time of Emperor Charles, who had such need of its help because of the wars that had taken place in Germany against the Lutherans and [because of] other most important expeditions."[9]

When de León looked at the Inca nation, he did not primarily see a culture with its own ways of living in relationship to the land, its own technologies, its own rituals and shared goods. He did not see land that was skillfully used and cared for. He did not, ultimately, see human beings bearing the divine image. Note that the world he was seeing was "not known by men." Rather, he interpreted what he saw purely in terms of how it could benefit him. While it is true that this is simply our natural temptation because of the pervasive effects of sin, it is also true that material circumstances can often be a powerful force to help us resist sin. It is always wrong to lie, but the average person is less likely to lie if the lie is likely to disrupt their daily experience of the world in some tangible, hard-hitting way. But when materiality is pushed to the margin and denied a voice, one protection against our natural selfishness is taken away.

And so these early Spanish conquistadores and explorers saw wealth that could be made useful in the wars of King Charles, who was then the holy Roman emperor and king of Spain. Jennings argues that the fundamental habit of mind betrayed by such words has become pervasive in the modern West—the mind of conquest and colonialism. It is a spirit that rejects the ontological density of the world, replacing it with a kind of empty, naked "matter." Tolkien called this mentality "a mind of metal and gears" and critiques it relentlessly in his treatment of the character of Saruman in *The Lord of the Rings*. Indeed, near the end of his life, he told a group of admirers that he saw "many many descendants of Saruman" in the world.[10] It has become the default way that most of us engage the world around us.

When the Europeans arrived in the New World, they chose to identify themselves in ways that broke that essential bond between the body and the earth—they had left their own home places behind, after all. Brunner's suspension bridge collapsed, as one side was torn down and the other was asked to bear more weight than it was meant to. Rather than choosing to align their lives with the life of these new places, the early colonialists chose instead to exploit them, to take from them. This act had the effect of not only breaking *their* bonds to the land but also breaking the complex web of relationships that had existed between the Native peoples and their land. Jennings explains,

> The new worlds were transformed into land—raw, untamed land. And the European visions saw these new lands as a system of potentialities, a mass of undeveloped and unused potentialities. Everything—from peoples and their bodies to plants and animals, from the ground and the sky—was subject to change, subjects for change, subjected to change. The significance of this transformation cannot be overstated. The earth itself was barred from being a constant signifier of identity. Europeans defined Africans and all others apart from the earth even as they separated them from their lands.

The central effect of the loss of the earth as an identity signifier was that Native identities—tribal, communal, familial, and spatial— were constricted to simply their bodies, leaving behind the very ground that enables and facilitates the articulation of identity. The profound commodification of bodies that was New World slavery signifies an effect humankind has yet to reckon with fully—a distorted vision of creation.[11]

The problems we see today, in which so many of our friends and neighbors seem withdrawn from each other, are rooted in the advent of the colonial modern world and are inextricably tied to questions of race and justice. It was colonialism that helped normalize this idea that the people, animals, and plants that I encounter in the world do not contribute to my identity in any way but can be made useful to me as I seek to create my own identity. When the colonialists came to these new lands and uprooted the lives of the Native peoples, an essential bond was broken between people and place, so that human identity had to be refashioned apart from history, culture, and land.

THE REVOLUTION WAS WHITE

What was left for making human identities? There are two answers to this question, both of which are significant for understanding the rootlessness and alienation endemic in our time.

First, we were left with our bodies. Culture was denied a voice in shaping identity. Language was denied a voice. Landscapes and geography were denied a voice. Imagine trying to identify yourself to another person but not being allowed to cite your hometown, your family, your cultural practices and habits, and so on. What do you have left to appeal to, given all that has been taken away? You are left with your body. Jennings says, "Without place as the articulator of identity, human skin was asked to fly solo and speak for itself."[12]

Making a similar point, the Standing Rock Sioux theologian Vine Deloria Jr. wrote,

> The white man, where viewed in this context, appears as a perennial adolescent. He is continually moving about, and his restless nature cannot seem to find peace. Yet *he does not listen to the land* and so cannot find a place for himself. He has few relatives and seems to believe that the domestic animals that have always relied upon him constitute his only link with the other peoples of the universe. Yet he does not treat these animals as friends but only as objects to be exploited. While he has destroyed many holy places of the Indians, he does not seem to be able to content himself with his own holy places.[13]

Given this perspective, the eventual racial outworking of the problem begins to make more sense. After all, who managed this transition to an individualist world "better" than anyone else (if we measure success by the acquisition of wealth and power)? It was mostly Europeans, and more specifically—especially after the sixteenth century—fair-skinned northern Europeans. Thus when human beings were forced to view themselves chiefly as detached, isolated selves, the body became a natural signifier of identity. And in this world, the bodies of the exploiters—the bodies of White people—appeared to be the most successful and thus superior.

Likewise, the bodies of darker-skinned people, consistently exploited and used as raw material by Whites, came to be regarded as less valuable, and even less human.

As a result, "whiteness" began to emerge as a way of making sense of human identity. To be "White" was to be capable of imposing your will onto the world around you through force, to seize what you desired, and to claim the life you wanted. It was, Jennings argues, a "framework for human maturity." To be "mature" in the colonial world—that is, to be a fully realized human person—was to possess the degree of power and agency typified by White people, and especially by White men.

For the Europeans, whiteness became an identity to preserve and live into—it was the identity of successful individualists who managed to create identities of wealth, status, and power by "projecting meaning into the world," to use Jennings's phrase. But for darker-skinned peoples, whiteness became something they were meant to aspire to. Defined this way, whiteness is inclusive: anybody can become "White," provided they possess the talent and will needed to subdue land and people to their will. Thus maturity, or a kind of fully realized life—a successful life—came to be defined in racial terms.

This identifying of maturity with race would persist for centuries. In 1957, when Ghana became the first free postcolonial state in sub-Saharan Africa, Western politicians and journalists descended on the new nation's capital city of Accra to join the independence celebration. Anne Fremantle, an American writer covering the event for the *New York Times*, said that the occasion was "a living witness to the success of the White Fathers' work and enduring results."[14] American vice president Richard Nixon, who was also in attendance, would sound a similar note, saying that "here in Ghana we have as good an example of a colonial policy at its best as the world can see."[15] Whiteness was maturity. For people of color to become complete, they needed to become like their European conquerors.

This reality would inform the way White people approached their relationships to people of color. People who were thought to be incapable of achieving maturity or less likely to become mature were condemned to forever remain no more than a raw good to be consumed and used for the prosperity of the mature. Likewise, if White people sought to help people of color achieve maturity, virtually anything could be justified in service of that goal.

In a particularly disgraceful chapter of American history, "reformer" Richard Pratt, a key figure in the establishing of boarding schools that sought to Americanize the country's Native peoples, explained to the United States Congress that his work was a ministry of mercy. According to Pratt, it was the "Indian" in each Native person that was the danger. "Kill the Indian in him to save the man," Pratt told the Congress.[16] In the White vision of human maturity, the Native person could never become mature as long as he remained recognizably Native—while he dressed in the clothing of his people, spoke their language, and lived a life closely tied to the land in the traditions of his people. To become mature, he needed to be lifted up by the White Americans. And so, perfectly functional, life-giving tribal societies were destroyed, and children were taken from their families and put into boarding schools where they were beaten if they were caught speaking their mother tongue. All this could be justified because it was clearing the way toward the objective that the Native peoples of the Americas could eventually become mature, which meant "autonomous, self-realized individuals."

What is especially jarring is to realize that there were some Christians who understood what was happening, spoke up against it, and warned of the consequences. Herman Bavinck was one of them. In an address given in 1911 while he was a member of the Dutch parliament, Bavinck warned his listeners of what would happen if the work of foreign missions was tied to the colonial project. Bavinck feared that European culture, with its rationalism and consumerist tendencies, was quite hostile to Christian faith. Moreover, because colonialism was outsourcing the West's *actual* value system of colonialism rather than Christianity, the melding of Christianity with colonialism could only bring disaster. "Colonialism's influence unraveled a rich and ancient tapestry of native non-Western beliefs about this world and the next," author and professor James Eglinton explains. "And offered nothing more to take its place than the already threadbare chintz of secular consumerism."[17]

Unfortunately, Bavinck's warning was not heard. And we are still living with the consequences. In time, the animating spirit behind the colonial project would become universalized, as everything in creation outside of sovereign individual selves would be reduced to mere matter. There may be no clearer expression of it than the much-critiqued words of Justice Kennedy: "Central to the idea of liberty is the right to define one's own concept of existence." The colonialists themselves couldn't have said it better. We have lost the inheritance and replaced it with a blind grasping after power and security and wealth.

In an essay called "The Iliad, or the Poem of Force," the French mystic Simone Weil defines *force* as a power that transforms human persons—in all their uniqueness, personal richness, and subjectivity—into objects. Force is "that x that turns anybody who is subjected to it into a thing." She says that ultimately the most obvious form force can take is killing, "for it turns a man into a thing in the most literal sense: it makes a corpse of him." Yet it may also be the case, Weil suggests, that blunt force of this kind is actually the least horrifying:

> How much more varied in its processes, how much more surprising in its effects is the other force, the force that does *not* kill, i.e., that does not kill just yet. It will surely kill, it will possibly kill, or perhaps it merely hangs, poised and ready, over the head of the creature it *can* kill, at any moment, which is to say at every moment. In whatever aspect, its effect is the same: it turns a man into a stone. From its first property (the ability to turn a human being into a thing by the simple method of killing him) flows another, quite prodigious too in its own way, the ability to turn a human being into a thing while he is still alive.[18]

Because of the twin effect produced by this particular vision of maturity and the centrality of force in the colonial mind, the modern world was shaped by destructive and dehumanizing tendencies that have wreaked havoc on the world and on countless human communities across the globe ever since.

THE DANGEROUS SIN OF UNBELIEF

What is the core failure of this vision of nature that centers on force and privileges the individual who possesses wealth and the ability to self-designate? In one sense, its chief problem is the sin of pride. So confident were these White colonialists in their own superiority to the people they encountered that they did not feel it was necessary to listen to them or to learn from their ways of living in what was, to the Europeans, a strange new place, and what was, to the Indigenous peoples, their home. Pride gives an excess of confidence, a sense that we need not listen to what another says because we are already wise.

That said, there is a deeper sin that reaches back behind pride toward something more basic, even visceral. When we are proud, we believe something about ourselves that is not true. The story of Nebuchadnezzar in Daniel 4 is representative of much modern thinking: we survey our world—our home, our job, our bank account—and say, "Is not this great Babylon, which I have built?" The trouble is that ultimately our accomplishments are not our own, at least not entirely. They are achieved with the benefits of caring and supportive relationships, structures and laws, employees and coworkers, and so on.

More basic still, all our accomplishments are done breathing air with lungs that God gave us and eating food that grows thanks to light, air, and water—none of which is something that you and I, or any other human being, can make. The bare fact of our existence as human creatures testifies that we are not autonomous, self-designating individuals. The regime of force persists because we refuse to believe this fact that is hardwired into our lives as finite beings. In ignoring the testimony of nature and neighbor on their arrival in the New World, the European Christians left behind an example of indifference to revelation that continues to haunt the American church to this day. So the chief sin at issue in this indifference is not actually pride but *unbelief*. God has disclosed himself to us through his created world, through our neighbors and through the land, but we have not listened to the voice of creation.

In his book *Faith. Hope. Love.*, Mark Jones notes that unbelief is the first sin. It is the sin that first disrupted the primordial beauty of God's creation. And so the sin of the colonizers is a recapitulation of the sin that condemned humanity to its fallen state. Consider the account of Eve's temptation in Genesis 3. The serpent does not begin by tempting Eve to take the fruit and eat. He begins by tempting her to disbelieve what God has said. "Did God *actually* say?" he asks her. And in that question is the destruction of love and mutuality among people and the destruction of humane belonging in the created order. Eve chooses not to believe God but to believe the serpent instead. It should not surprise us then that the first sin would lead to many, *many* devastating consequences downstream.

This is how Jones describes it: "Unbelief is no small sin but rather the greatest of all sins. It gives birth to all other sins. Or to put the matter more vividly, unbelief essentially tells God to shut up, because we do not want to hear what he says. Just as faith brings us to God, so unbelief causes us to run from God."[19] And that, of course, is precisely what happened as the root sin of the colonizers took a deeper hold in the lives and imaginations of Western Christians and, in different ways, across the globe.

When we consider that God speaks to us not only through Scripture but also through nature, the relevance of the sin of unbelief to our common lives becomes more apparent. Telling God to "shut up" is not simply a matter of rejecting the Bible, as many often think. The Bible is not the only way God speaks to the world. As Bavinck notes in his *Reformed Dogmatics*, both the written testimony of Scripture and the less perceptible but still real divine disclosure found in the creation are forms of divine revelation. John Bolt, the editor of Bavinck's work, summarized the idea this way: "Creation

Revelation is no less supernatural than Scripture; in both, God himself is at work and his providential creating, sustaining, and governing form a single mighty ongoing revelation."[20]

To reject God's revelation of himself is not simply to reject the Bible—what some theologians have called the "book of Scripture." It is also to reject his communication to us through the created world, the "book of nature." The late Roman Catholic pope St. John Paul II makes the point well in his encyclical, *Evangelium Vitae*:

> When the sense of God is lost, the sense of man is also threatened and poisoned. . . . Moreover, once all reference to God has been removed, it is not surprising that the meaning of everything else becomes profoundly distorted. Nature itself, from being "mater" (mother), is now reduced to being "matter," and is subjected to every kind of manipulation. This is the direction in which a certain technical and scientific way of thinking, prevalent in present-day culture, appears to be leading when it rejects the very idea that there is a truth of creation which must be acknowledged, or a plan of God for life which must be respected.[21]

This helps explain why Western people have spent the past several hundred years wantonly desecrating God's world. If the regime of force began with unbelief, then the violent destruction of the created world is simply another way in which human beings, in Jones's vivid phrase, "tell God to shut up."

This is precisely the sort of movement Arendt describes that culminates in the space race. God gives to humanity a garden. People look at that garden and judge it to be a prison from which they must be emancipated. We have become like the dwarves at the end of C. S. Lewis's *The Last Battle*: we are surrounded by creaturely beauty and divine extravagance, but when a cup of fragrant wine is held to our nose, we sense only stale water from an animal's trough.[22]

This is why the sin of unbelief is so dangerous. Its consequences cannot be contained but ripple out into all of life, affecting our ability to perceive reality properly and to love what is given. This is why the laughter of Fr. Acosta would prove so deadly. This is why unbelief is the root sin of the modern West—though it would take this sin several centuries to work itself out more broadly beyond its horrifying origins at the beginning of the exploration and seizure of the Americas.

3

THE UNMAKING OF PLACES

The Fruit of Industrialism

In 1871 Buffalo Bill Cody, the famous showman of the old American West, stood on a bluff on the banks of the Platte River, only about thirty minutes from my home in Lincoln, Nebraska. He was accompanied by a half dozen wealthy New Yorkers out to see the "old West" with the man who had done more to make it famous than anyone else.

And they did see Cody's old West—if not the true West. It was a hunting expedition, and a well-armed one at that. Writing in *The Atlantic*, J. Weston Phippen describes the extravagant traveling party that these men brought with them from the East Coast: "The Army had supplied an armed escort and 25 wagons filled with cooks, linen, china, carpets for their tents, and a traveling icehouse to keep their wine chilled."[1] It wasn't just the accommodations that were extravagant. The men had also made a bet that the first man to bring down a buffalo would win a silver cup.

As they stood on the bluff surveying the lands around, Cody spotted six bison on a plain two miles away. They approached slowly from downwind so as not to alert the buffalo to their presence. Once they were close enough, they charged. One of the hunters described what happened next, reporting that they eventually killed a number of buffalo. Each hunter would take the tail as a prize to mark his conquest and then some of the best meat. The rest they would leave to rot in the sun.[2]

Once boasting a population of more than thirty million buffalo that dotted the prairies, by 1900 the Great Plains were home to only a few hundred. By the measures of Cody and his friends, this was a great success. Killing the buffalo and leaving them to rot was how Cody and others could clear the way for the resettling of the plains, driving the Omaha and Pawnee tribes off their lands and replacing them with self-sufficient, independent farmers ready to take a slice of what might be described as the great North American cake. (That is precisely the term that Belgian king Leopold II used to describe the sub-Saharan African lands and resources European colonists were set on stealing at roughly the same time.) One contemporary stated the point as starkly as one can imagine: "Every buffalo dead is an Indian gone."[3] And a contemporary scholar said of the destruction of the buffalo that "European colonization of the Americas treats animals and wildlife as this congress of resources. We make them into commodities that we can exploit at our whim."[4]

This is the natural evolution of the view of nature described in the previous chapter. This vision of the world could not simply be arrested by the conquest of the Incas, Aztecs, and other Indigenous groups in the sixteenth century. The violence done to the people who loved the land would inevitably be enacted on the land and animals themselves.

In many accounts of Christianity's confrontation with modernity, the drama takes place mostly in the realm of ideas—which, as we are often told, "have consequences." But while there is something true in that account, it leaves a lot out. In particular, it tends to push the material circumstances to the edge of the story, along with the desires and motivations that shape the world just as profoundly as the ideas.

Certainly we ought to understand Nietzsche and Freud and Marx and many other philosophers and thinkers if we are to understand our era. But we also need to understand men like Cody—

entertainers who simply thought they were in a business, doing their job, and making a livelihood for themselves. Never mind the cost to the land or to the people that depended on it—that wasn't the point. The point was clearing the way for White settlers to arrive, to bring civilization and prosperity to the Great Plains. The actual characteristics of the land were irrelevant. The needs of the land and the animals that lived off it were irrelevant. In time, even the needs of the poor White farmers who came to the plains, such as my Swedish immigrant ancestors who arrived here a decade after Cody's hunt, would be judged irrelevant too. All that mattered was making the land suitable to the shape of American ambition.

THE LOGIC OF THE REVOLUTION

By the late nineteenth century the underlying logic of the colonial mind had begun to work itself out. The genocide of Native peoples was well under way in North America, as both whole people groups and the ecosystems they understood and submitted themselves to were destroyed.

Meanwhile, Africa too was being ravaged by colonial explorers. In a particularly telling moment, future prime minister of the United Kingdom Lord Salisbury, returning from the Conference of Berlin, where European leaders had divided up the African continent into separate colonies for their control and use, said, "We have been giving away mountains and rivers and lakes to each other, only hindered by the small impediment that we never knew exactly where they were."[5]

The European delegates at Berlin, much like Pedro de León, were unconcerned with the Indigenous life in Africa at the time. They saw simply a "dark continent" that ought to be made civilized and that, in the meantime, would make many powerful Europeans quite wealthy. The people groups of Africa, their cultures, their way of life, were all pushed to the margins while African peoples themselves were made to serve as the grist that powered the colonial mill.

However, by this time Europe herself had begun to feel the tremors caused by the onset of colonial modernity. It turns out that the colonial mind that denies full creaturely status to nature and neighbor cannot be contained or limited to only affect people of other racial groups or belonging to other places. Eventually it turns in on itself and creates discord and division among the colonialists themselves. So it was in Europe in the nineteenth century—and, slightly later, in America as well. The name that many of us have come to associate with this era is the "industrial revolution." It was a time when the earlier, older colonial revolution began to manifest itself in White society in both Europe and America. In time, it would take its toll on White society in much the same way that colonialism had on Indigenous communities in North America and Africa.

THE GREAT UNSETTLING

When we bother to talk about the industrial revolution today, we tend to remember it as a time when liberty blossomed in the world as new technology allowed for unprecedented improvements in GDP, life expectancy, general health, and quality of life. New machines made some forms of work easier and made it easier to produce more goods. The wealth this created did produce a number of positive outcomes. In his book *The Suicide of the West*, Jonah Goldberg argues that the beginning of the rapid improvement in material conditions for humanity dates back to industrialization. Likewise in her book on the industrial revolution, *Liberty's Dawn*, historian Emma Griffin argues that the industrial revolution that took place in eighteenth-century England produced an era of material, educational, and romantic flourishing across the nation as countless multitudes were freed from a life of being chained to the land and to toilsome work.

It is certainly true that there are improvements in our material lives that stem from the industrial revolution. The average life span grew. Infant mortality declined. In time, many deadly diseases became much less common thanks to modern sanitation and much less deadly thanks to modern medicine. The average person began to have more money. These were all genuine gains that should be celebrated.

In critiquing industrialism our goal should not be to reach back to some pre-industrial era but rather to do what all Christians must do: to assess the health of our society and its history according to Christian ideas of morality and justice. We cannot reach back to the days before these disastrous revolutions; we can only seek to live *through* them and come out on the other side with something healthier and more faithful that repudiates them. But just as it is wrong to endorse overly simple theories of cultural decline, it's also wrong to accept overly optimistic theories of cultural progression. Ambiguity reigns in human history, and it's a lesson that conservatives and progressives alike would do well to heed.

So it is with industrialization. It is essential that we understand the precise nature of the changes brought about during this time if we are to understand the complex world it created and how we continue to wrestle with it down through the present.

An illustration from J. R. R. Tolkien's *The Lord of the Rings* may be helpful here. Early in the story, the wizard Gandalf explains to the Hobbit Frodo what will happen to someone who possesses Sauron's ring for a long time. They will not die, Gandalf explains, but nor will they receive more life—they will simply go on. Eventually, this causes a sort of thinning, even a fading, of the person who possesses the ring. Their years have stretched far beyond their natural capacity, and so they themselves are physically stretched too, in time becoming almost transparent. While the ring's possessor still exists, something has nonetheless been lost as the natural shape of their life has been suppressed and then forgotten. Bilbo, who possessed the ring for many years, describes it by saying that he feels like "butter scraped over too much bread." He describes feeling "thin" just before he finally gives up the ring.[6]

Tolkien is suggesting that there's a way of extending one's *existence* without gaining more *life*. There's a difference, in other words, between mere existence and life itself. Existence is the simple fact of being in the world. Life, on the other hand, is existing in harmonious relationship with the world. The former is solitary, the latter communal; the former segregated, the latter integrated.

Understanding this difference is central to understanding the gains that have come from the Industrial Age. The English historian Christopher Dawson, himself a favorite of Tolkien's, describes the transformation brought about by industrialism this way: "The tendency of the Industrial Age was to consider reward rather than work, to judge everything in terms of money. Men worked in order to get rich, and the state of being rich was an absolute end which need not serve any other social purpose—a kind of Nirvana. In this, as in other things, that age subordinated the human to the material."[7] The process of industrialization proceeded by taking apart things that rightly belonged together. Work was no longer to fulfill a social function with a community, but to acquire money. It didn't matter if you acquired money in a way that assisted your neighbor or honored God or not. Dawson contrasts this with an older vision of work and society: "In the Middle Ages, and in many other periods of a more stable social order, social status was inseparable from function. The knight's land and the merchant's money existed like the endowments of the abbeys and colleges, in order to enable them to fulfill their office. A man who had great wealth and no function was an anomaly, and so also to a lesser degree was the man who had a function and no means to fulfill it."[8] In older times, Dawson suggests, people understood that there was a close relationship between a person's purpose within a community and their financial means. There was an indissoluble relationship between a person's work and their neighbor. Industrialism broke this relationship by severing the spiritual and communal realities of work from the financial gains of work.

The American Presbyterian J. Gresham Machen raised a similar concern in his classic book *Christianity and Liberalism*. While acknowledging that the material gains produced by industrialization are real, Machen lamented what industrialism had left out: "The modern world represents in some respects an enormous improvement over the world in which our ancestors lived; but in other respects it exhibits a lamentable decline. The improvement appears in the physical conditions of life, but in the spiritual realm there is a corresponding loss."[9] Later in that same section, Machen would say that modernity "concerns itself only with the production of physical well-being." That is a good distillation of Dawson and Machen's concern with the "progress" humanity achieved in the industrial revolution. It's also in keeping with the critique Jennings makes when he points out that, when nature and neighbor are transformed into "things," all that's left to define ourselves is our material body.

The material progress of the industrial revolution was real in a certain sense, as we've already acknowledged. But even in the early twentieth century, both Dawson and Machen were fearful of what the consequences of industrialism would be. Material lives were being extended and made more comfortable, but the spiritual needs of the human person were being squelched. They began to wonder whether we were actually acquiring more life or simply continuing to exist.

THE INDUSTRIAL REVOLUTION IN PRACTICE

The creation of new technologies, such as the steam engine, brought the end of certain lines of work, as well as the broader ways of living that existed around them. But what's more, by foregrounding the pursuit of material progress, especially wealth, and backgrounding harder to define spiritual concerns, industrialism was able to justify its disruptiveness by claiming that the wealth it produced would benefit everyone—even those who had lost their lines of work and local economies. The historian Kirkpatrick Sale describes it this way: "It was an economy, whatever else might be said about it, designed to unleash certain human appetites, greed not insignificant among them, and to enrich certain human endeavors, material amassment being primary."[10]

One example comes from the Luddite revolt in England in the early nineteenth century. When we hear the word *Luddite* today, we tend to think of a crankish figure, a recalcitrant technology hater bitterly clinging to their typewriter and rotary phone, refusing to see the progress technology has brought about. This portrayal actually tells us far more about the lovers of technological progress than it does about the flesh-and-blood Luddites of history. By considering the actual Luddites, a group of early nineteenth-century weavers in the English midlands and northwest, we can also better understand the way industrial technology transformed the human and geographic landscapes.

These original Luddites, whose name came from a fictitious leader of the movement named King Ludd, objected to the wide adoption of a new mechanical loom that produced far more cloth in much less time than a human weaver could. This new loom gave the factory owners, who were wealthy enough to afford such technology, an enormous advantage over the small home-based enterprises that had been more common up until that time.

The weavers of the English midlands knew that the new loom would mean the end of their way of life. And they were right. Hundreds, if not thousands, of men who had owned their own businesses and used their work to create a certain way of life for their families, neighborhoods, and cities were suddenly driven out of business.

For many of these men, now deprived of their livelihood but still having families to provide for, their only option for employment was to go to work for the very factory owners who had used their machines to drive them out of work. And the conditions in which these owners forced them to work were often horrifying.

What's worse, because the pay in these mills was so poor, it was not uncommon for women and children to also be forced to work in them just so a family could make ends meet. Sale describes the conditions in some of the early-nineteenth-century cotton mills, noting that workers faced twelve- to fourteen-hour days, sometimes even eighteen-hour days, and could have wages docked for everything from having a window open to whistling to being five minutes late to work. Moreover, factory owners routinely employed foremen whose main duty was to beat people who were late to their work or fell asleep on the job. The most frequent targets for such treatment were women and children, and, Sale reports, some children were beaten so severely they died from their injuries.[11]

Though Sale doesn't mention it, it's worth noting that the cotton these Luddites were working with in the mills most commonly came from the southern United States, grown and harvested by slave labor. And so the cotton business was one extended injustice, aided and abetted by the combination of white supremacy, an all-too-typical capitalist indifference to human suffering, and techno-logical means that aided the capitalist class in their work. Thus what animated the Luddites was neither a simple reactionary ten-dency that caused them to hate technology nor a naive romanticism about the past. They were enraged by genuine injustices that were having horrific consequences for their way of life. The issue wasn't the machinery but, as Sale says, "what the machinery stood for." The workers saw their lives being stripped away and transformed into something ugly and inhuman, so they rebelled.

The Luddites became more and more desperate—and even-tually more and more violent. What began as nighttime raids to smash the machines would become attacks on the factory owners and the politicians that supported them. When one such owner was killed, popular opinion turned against the Luddites and their cause was defeated. Their story has, perhaps predictably, been lost to history. Yet the fears and concerns that drove Luddite activism have, if anything, been largely vindicated by the past two hundred years of history.

Industrialism produced other similar stories as well. In the early 1800s in New York, a union of shoemakers sued factory owners on grounds that the owners were refusing to pay them a fair wage and were using unqualified, under-skilled workers to replace them and suppress wages. The factory owners, for their part, responded by suing the shoemakers for trying to deny those less qualified workers their right to work. As John Lauritzen Larson notes in his book *The Market Revolution in America*, both sides of the debate thought they were contending for "freedom." The questions, as they ever are, were, Freedom for who? Freedom to what end? Freedom for the workers to pursue a way of life that was fruitful and served the needs of their families? Or freedom for the owners to pursue profit?

In these rival conceptions of freedom we can see the older humane values set against the materialistic values of the industrial revolution. This was not merely a fight over wages. The shoemakers were not simply after better pay. They were trying to maintain a way of living that suited them and their families in which work was an integrated part that suited whole communities. In Dawson's terms, they wanted the wages they needed to fulfill their function within society.

The factory owners, in contrast, saw freedom as chiefly about the freedom to make money—the overlap with Jennings's conception of whiteness should be obvious. Because the shoemakers' strike was threatening their freedom to do that, the shoemakers were depriving the owners, as well as the other less skilled workers that were not striking, of their basic right to work.

Industrialism took place because tools were being invented that would permanently transform human society. But these tools—and the men who owned them and used them to enrich themselves—were themselves indifferent to the shape of society and to the needs of human persons. Technology itself is nearly always indifferent to such things, but even so the specific nature of a technology will lend itself toward certain uses and habits of thought. The machinery of industrialism tended toward efficiency at the expense of virtually all other values and concerns—a tendency that was shared by the owners of the machinery. To return to Dawson and Machen, this is all a story of how the material has overtaken the spiritual, leaving human beings detached from one another and alienated from the world.

TECHNOLOGY'S PLACE IN COMMON LIFE

This critique of the industrial era can and must be distinguished from a more blanket sort of nostalgia for a past without public health, modern plumbing, and so on. We can imagine ways that industrial technology could have been adapted so that it still improved efficiency but without such dire consequences for common life.

It's not simply that these new tools disrupted older ways of working. That's inherent in any new technological development—the advent of sailing ships, for example, disrupted older forms of ship making. The point is that these new forms of technology were designed to maximize financial gains for the people who owned them by providing for consumer needs and were mostly indifferent to the broader needs of the human person related to social life, work, and so on.

In other words, the problem of the industrial revolution was not the machines per se. It was, rather, that these machines functioned according to the revolutionary logic we have already described: they were ordered to acquire wealth and power as goods in themselves. Beyond that, the only concern was producing goods cheaply so that they could be sold cheaply. While this concern does provide a narrow benefit for individual consumers, it comes at a high cost as the health of the land is jeopardized and the broader needs of human communities are ignored.

None of this means that technology itself is bad or disordered. Technology is the fruit of human work and creativity. When the human mind is used to produce goods that are of service to neighbor and family, God is glorified. The problem is with the production of tools that work with an essential indifference to the broader needs of the human community and of the land itself.

The Catholic philosopher Romano Guardini explains that the problem is not between people who hate technology and people who like the comforts of modern life. Rather, the question is what kind of technologies we will make, how we will use them, and how they will shape us. He compares two methods of traveling over water—the sailing ship and the ocean liner. He notes that a sailing ship, though it is a human technology, is a kind of technology that exists in close relationship to nature: "Those who control this ship are still very closely related to the wind and waves. They are breast to breast with their force. Eye and hand and whole body brace against them. We have here real culture—elevation above nature, yet decisive nearness to it. We are still in a vital way body, but we are shot through with mind and spirit. We master nature by the power of mind and spirit, but we ourselves remain natural."[12]

There is no problem with technology itself. Human beings are makers. Indeed, the Christian believes that God gave to humanity a high calling to steward the earth. Stewardship implies power and control, but a particular kind of power, one that is oriented not only toward the advancement of the one possessing power but toward the health and prosperity of those under that person's care.

So the Christian critique of industrialism can never be antitechnological. It cannot flow from a desire to return to a pristine world free from all technology—that world never existed. Rather, the Christian calling is to steward the world toward the ends God has for it, which is a city marked by plentitude and joy. So the calling is not to be antitechnology but to be opposed to the kinds of technology that achieve their gains by neglecting or even harming parts of reality. We need not become Amish, in other words, but we would likely do well to, in the phrase of Andy Crouch, become "almost Amish."[13]

The modern idea of "progress" sees technological development as a means of emancipating people to become their authentic selves. But this leaves us with very limited opportunity to critique new forms of technology, since more powerful, robust, or efficient tools can only mean more powerful, robust, or efficient people. A Christian approach to technology, in contrast, allows us to treat each technological development individually, asking each time why the tool is needed, what values it will impart to its users, and how it will shape the imagination of society more generally.

Guardini flips the conversation about technology on its head when he suggests that we ought to approach technology with a certain skepticism. Commonly, when the merits of a particular tool are debated, it's assumed that the burden of proof rests with the skeptic. The assumption is that our predilection should be to favor the creation and production of new technology and only in extreme cases reject new forms of it.

But Guardini suggests that we ought to take the opposite approach, defaulting to current practices and demanding that the technologist furnish the proof that a new tool should be promoted across society. He grants that the creation of ocean liners is "a brilliant technological achievement," and yet he thinks that something important is lost with such ships.

> A colossus of this type presses on through the sea regardless of wind and waves. It is so large that nature no longer has power over it; we can no longer see nature on it. People on board eat and drink and sleep and dance. They live as if in houses and on city streets. Something decisive has been lost here. Not only has there been step-by-step development, improvement, and increase in size; a fluid line has been crossed that we cannot fix precisely but can only detect when we have long since passed over it—a line on the far side of which living closeness to nature has been lost. While that original example of human culture which we called a boat or a ship was a work of the mind and spirit, it was also fully integrated into nature. That type of culture, constantly fashioned afresh by the vital action and movement of the whole person, is no longer with us.[14]

What kind of world did industrialism create? We must understand that, as Sale put it, industrialism is not simply a model for production of goods; it is a culture. In particular, it is the sort of culture that tends toward the view that human beings can do anything through industry if only we would remove the limits that have traditionally constrained our behavior.

This should sound familiar. The discovery that old limits no longer apply, that we can take what we desire without concern for nature or neighbor, did not begin with industrialism. It began in Eden, of course, when Eve refused to believe God. But this tendency took a new shape when the colonists encountered the strange new peoples and landscapes of the Americas. The spirit that defined their response to that encounter is also the spirit that defines industrialism. It is a profoundly dangerous spirit—even a demonic one. Sale explains it well:

Imagine . . . what happens to a culture when it actually de-velops the means to transcend limits, making it possible and therefore right to destroy custom and community, to create new rules of employment and obligation, to magnify pro-duction and consumption, to impose new means and ways of work, and to control or ignore the central forces of nature. It would no doubt exist for quite a long time, powerful and ex-pansionary and prideful, before it had to face up to the truths that it was founded upon an illusion and that there are real limits in an ordered world, social and economic as well as natural, that ought not be transgressed, limits more important than their conquest.[15]

We today do not need to imagine, of course. It's the world we live in—and it's a world that has become uniquely alienating. Yet as we will see in the next chapter, the tragic response many in the West offered to the alienation of the industrial revolution did not ac-tually address the problem. Rather, it was a further step toward universalizing whiteness. If industrialism was an unmaking of the land, what came next was the unmaking of human bodies.

4

THE UNMAKING
OF THE BODY

Considering the Sexual Revolution

The woman that history knows only as Señora J. G. was thirty years old when she visited the clinic. She already had ten children, ranging in age from ten months to sixteen years. Her husband, according to author Margaret Marsh, "drank heavily and insisted on daily intercourse but claimed to be too ill to work."[1] This woman had come to the clinic to participate in a study on a birth control pill overseen by American scientists. It was the mid-1950s in Puerto Rico, and within a few short years, the pill would make its debut in both the United States and the United Kingdom.

But before it hit markets there, American scientists traveled to Puerto Rico to find human test subjects for the drug. American women had been offered the chance to test the drug, but those experiments did not last long because of "difficulties in recruiting enough women to take part in the trial and high drop-out rates because of the side effects."[2] As had happened before in American medicine, medical "progress" came at the expense of people of color.[3] And so it would in Puerto Rico.

Many of the women recruited to test the drug were college students who were threatened with bad grades if they refused to participate.

Moreover, the women who took the drug were not told that it was still in development, nor were they warned of the potential side effects. And side effects there were: during the experiments, three women would die, and around 20 percent would report side effects such as headaches, weight gain, nausea, and dizziness.[4]

Yet these factors did not dissuade developers of the drug from releasing it in the United States. When the first version of the pill, known as Enovid, hit markets in America in 1960, it had only been tested on 130 people. Even in those days, this was not judged a sufficient sample for market release. So the scientists who developed the drug fudged the numbers. They would talk about how they had observed nearly 1,300 menstrual cycles during the development or note that they had distributed 40,000 pills. Both these claims were true—but they had still only tested it on 130 people.

That didn't stop the pill from forever transforming life in the Western world. In her memoirs of working as a midwife in postwar London, Jennifer Worth describes how the pill transformed her work: "In the late 1950s we had eighty to a hundred deliveries a month on our books. In 1963 the number had dropped to four or five a month."[5] That's a 200 percent decrease in births in just one part of one city.

Long-term concerns with the drug persisted well into the 1980s, when American drug companies debuted a new form of the pill with reduced hormone levels that seems to have reduced or eliminated many of its long-term health risks.

None of this sordid history proves anything about how contraception ought to be approached today, to be sure. To live in the world at all is to enter midway into a story that has already seen great evil. To be an American is to receive an inheritance that includes rampant racism, manifested most obviously (though not exclusively) to African Americans and Native Americans. It is impossible to extricate ourselves fully from cycles of violence that came before us. If we were to try, we would have to withdraw from the world altogether, and even then we would likely still fail. If the horrific roots of the pill made all contraception illegitimate, what else would have to fall by that principle?

Even so, there is something we ought to note here. By the mid-twentieth century, the life of households had so degraded that many women felt the need to be emancipated from them. The home had ceased to be a place of shared labor, productivity, and family life. It had instead become a kind of consumption center and storage hub—the lives of men and older children were largely spent outside of it. Women remained behind to manage what little remained of the household's life. It is not surprising, then, that many women found this life alienating, even in relatively functional situations. If you add to this story the abuse that a woman like Señora J. G. labored under, it's even easier to be sympathetic to the alienation felt by many women in midcentury America. Something vital in the human spirit had been squelched in many American women in the aftermath of industrialism and the dismembering of the American home. It was this exact sense of aimlessness that prompted Betty Friedan to write her generation-defining book *The Feminine Mystique*.

But our society's solution to the despair felt by many women was not to rethink the excesses of industrialism, to take steps to return the household to its rightful place, or to call husbands back toward their homes and communities back toward wholeness and belonging. It was not to reject the value system of industrialism that judged the value of work purely on the basis of its financial output. It was not to question the narrative that had shaped how new technology transformed society and changed our relationship to place and family. It was not to seek greater integration between human persons and nature, or to work to create conditions that might promote stronger bonds of membership between people that could unite communities and restore this lost vitality.

It was, rather, to double down on violence—to use the same brutal methods of industrialism that had severed the bond between husbands and household so that women could likewise be "emancipated." That this could only be done by rendering a woman's body sterile in the same way as a man's suggests that there is something in colonial modernity that is hostile to life, hostile to the body, even hostile to women.

It was out of this world that the sexual revolution was born. The sexual revolution beheld the emerging dystopia brought about by industrialism and determined that the best solution would be, to borrow a phrase from Jonathan Chait, to make an egalitarian dystopia.[6]

THE CASE FOR THE SEXUAL REVOLUTION

The sexual revolution is usually hailed as a key moment in the emancipation of women and LGBTQ+ individuals from the hateful repression of the patriarchal postwar world. Journalist John Heidenry describes it as "a time of great courage, genius, inspired wackiness, and steady vision." He sees the sexual revolution as pivotal in helping humanity to finally obtain "peace on earth."[7]

This isn't surprising. The key ideas about sexuality prevalent in the West today are that sex is essential to the good life, that everyone has the right to have sex with whomever they want (assuming the consent of all involved parties) without intrusion or interference from others, and that our right to love whomever we want is actually a central element of expressing our authentic selves. All these ideas, so central to how modern identities are formed and understood, are tied inextricably to the societal transformations that happened during the sexual revolution.

It's important to give this positive account of the sexual revolution its due, for there are many understandable reasons why it happened. We have already talked about how industrialization transformed the way Western people worked. The many tradespeople who maintained small businesses out of their homes—a system that united households and gave fathers and mothers and children good work to do together—were crushed by the increased efficiency afforded by the new machinery. These machines not only drove many people out of business—they also left many of these craftspeople with few employment options. Most commonly, they would end up working in the factories that had caused them to lose their livelihoods in the first place.

It was not unusual for these factories to employ not only men but women and children as well. Indeed, the nineteenth century was a uniquely bleak time for many workers, especially children. William Blake's poem "The Chimney Sweeper" is a suitably grim and accurate account of the life of many children under industrialism.[8] The plight of women was often little better. The evolution away from productive households and economies organized around those households deprived many people of a stable place for living, as well as condemning them to difficult and dangerous work in factories.

In time, of course, this picture began to change. Work conditions improved in the West, often because the most unpleasant and dangerous work was outsourced to the Majority World, though sometimes for other reasons too. Then pay began to climb. Along with better pay for workers, which made it possible for wives and children to return home, came the arrival of many modern conveniences and the growing accessibility of consumer goods. It was, for example, no longer necessary for families to make their own clothing in their homes. As clothing prices went down, thanks to the advent of industrial technology, the labor that needed to be done at home was diminished.

But with all these materially beneficial changes came a subtle redefining of the home. Work became defined by the *income* it produced rather than the *product* it produced. It came to mean little more than, "things a person does to make money." And so, the rewards of the financially obsessed industrial revolution came mostly to men, who had opportunity to work outside the home. Women, precisely because their ability to give birth tied them more tangibly to the life of the world, were often left behind, doing unpaid work that required less skill than in previous ages and that often came with far greater degrees of isolation. Industrialism had improved the financial lives of men, though at the cost of integral home living. But most women only felt the latter half of that story: they felt the disruption of the home, the disappearance of skilled and socially admired work, and the loneliness that often accompanied it, especially as, in the postwar world, more and more American families moved into suburban neighborhoods, which took them away from their broader families. They mostly did not feel the financial benefits or increased personal freedom enjoyed by successful professional men in postwar America.

By the 1960s it had become clear that all this "progress" had come at a terrible cost. Betty Friedan describes it well in *The Feminine Mystique*. The opening lines are justly famous as a clear depiction of the problem:

> The problem lay buried, unspoken, for many years in the minds of American women. It was a strange stirring, a sense of dissatisfaction, a yearning that women suffered in the middle of the twentieth century in the United States. Each suburban wife struggled with it alone. As she made the beds, shopped for groceries, matched slipcover material, ate peanut butter sandwiches with her children, chauffeured Cub Scouts and Brownies, lay beside her husband at night—she was afraid to ask even of herself the silent question—"Is this all?"[9]

This was one of the most obvious and sympathetic reasons for the sexual revolution: industrialism had gutted the household which had been the seat of communal life and the primary place where we could attempt good work together and give and receive love. This hollowing of the household came as a tradeoff: work became more efficient, in a very specific sense, and worker wages grew accordingly.

Yet in practice, many of the benefits of this trade flowed primarily to men and many of the costs were felt primarily by women. There were extreme cases, such as that of Señora J. G., but what most concerned Friedan was not those cases, sad as they were. Friedan's concerns skewed toward the less extreme but more numerous women whose lives looked relatively comfortable, yet who found themselves trapped in a life they had not anticipated or knowingly chosen.

The question that occupied Friedan and many others was this: What could be done to ensure that the socially valued work available to men, which compensated them well and offered a life of connection and purpose, could also be enjoyed by women? How could the playing field be leveled such that women would have the same opportunities as men to enjoy good work and maintain a satisfying life outside of the home, which was increasingly marginal in the social experience of many Americans?

The most obvious answer to this question, for scientific researchers and theorists alike, was to remove obstacles that prevented women from living such a life. And, so the story went, the greatest and most obvious obstacle was a woman's ability to become pregnant. Pregnancy would mean not only substantial changes to her body but also severe constraints on her time, as she would be the baby's primary caregiver, given that only she could nurse the baby, and thus on call 24/7. If a woman was pregnant or nursing, simple bodily factors dramatically constrained what kind of work she could do and how she could progress professionally, particularly since she was nearly always competing against people who did not have those same restrictions. The obvious path toward equality, in the logic of the industrial revolution, was contraception. Industry had broken the bonds that tied men to the household. Contraception would now do the same for women.

Is a world that requires the suppression of life to advance equality a world worth building? A few raised this concern. The Roman Catholic Church has been a longtime critic of contraception, partly on these grounds. Likewise, Herman Bavinck warned about these issues in his book on the Christian family. But these were voices crying in the wilderness. After all, much of the development of modernity up through the sexual revolution had already hinged on precisely this exchange: a willingness to suppress or even eliminate some forms of life for the benefit of other forms of life.

This was the story of colonialism, in which whole cultures were destroyed almost overnight for the enrichment of White Europeans. It was the story of industrialism, in which whole economies and the ways of life they engendered were likewise obliterated, to say nothing of the animals and landscapes that were also destroyed. The wide-scale acceptance of both contraception and abortion during the sexual revolution can be viewed as simply taking ideas about the human person that had been in the air for several centuries and applying them to sexuality—and in particular to women's bodies.

What the sexual revolution did, up to and including the broad acceptance of contraception and abortion, was make it easier for women to become, in Jennings's phrase, "centered selves," in the same way that most men were. The question that was seldom asked was whether becoming a centered self was a good thing for anyone, man or woman.

SEX IN THE CITY—OR THE COSMOS?

One way of understanding what happened in the sexual revolution is to see it as a reversion to certain pre-Christian norms. In his book *From Shame to Sin*, Kyle Harper argues that the signature shift in how Christianity affected attitudes about sexuality was the domain in which Christianity placed sexual ethics. The classical world situated sexual ethics in the life of a political society, such as a city. The morality of any sexual behavior was judged by how that behavior reinforced or undermined the political stability of Roman society.

This meant that all sorts of highly exploitative or brutal sexual behaviors were tolerated in the classical world because they either did not undermine social order or, in some cases, were even thought to reinforce social order. The existence of millions of de facto sex slaves throughout the empire was viewed as a social good because it was only through the existence of those slaves that the voracious sexual appetites of propertied Roman men could be contained. Without the slaves, it was thought, those energies would be turned toward pursuits much more likely to lead to societal instability, or even to unwanted and expensive wars.

Thus in the Roman world, sexual behavior was largely judged by how it affected the overall stability of the empire. Christianity's chief challenge to the classical world's sexual ethics was to replace the city with the cosmos. Christianity claimed that the morality of sexual acts was conditioned not by their relationship to the social norms and hierarchy of the city but by their fittingness with the world as it was made by God. Christianity allowed people to look at the millions of slaves throughout the empire—to say nothing of the women whose husbands kept a veritable harem of male and female partners on the side—and say, "This is wrong and has to stop," without much regard for the supposedly "essential" benefits this injustice provided. It gave them the boldness to make claims that, applied consistently, would change Roman society to such a degree that what came next would be unrecognizable compared to what came before.

In one sense, the sexual ethics of the post-Christian West of the twenty-first century could not be more different from the classical world of the first through fourth centuries. The classical world assumed that male sexual energy was basically boundless and that the stability of the city relied on finding ways to direct and discipline that energy. This meant that for men any number of sexual acts were admissible—anything from marital sex to keeping a female mistress to keeping a few young boys around to rape. Female slaves and young boys were seen as acceptable containers for a man's sexual energy that could not be satisfied in marriage. One Roman man crudely explained the role of slaves in Roman sexuality this way: "If your loins are swollen, and there's some home born slave boy or girl around where you can quickly stick it, would you rather burst with tension? Not I—I like an easy lay."[10] The only firm prohibition for the sexual behaviors of powerful men was to not have sexual relationships with the wives of other powerful men, since this would disrupt the life of the city by raising questions about the legitimacy of a man's heirs. The sexual well-being of virtually everyone else was a matter of no concern. In this way the spirit of the sexual revolution, with the premium it puts on consent, is sharply at odds with the sexual ideals of the classical world.

But there are also surprising resonances between the classical world and the post–sexual revolution West. First, in both the classical West and the sexual revolution, sex is assumed to be so basic and elemental to human life that you can't really do without it. The sexual revolution simply put the sexual energies of heterosexual women (and, in time, LGBTQ+ individuals) on the same level as heterosexual men. Indeed, one of the key factors in sparking the sexual revolution was the research of Drs. Alfred Kinsey and Bill Masters into the sexual lives of women. The sexual revolution was, in part, justified on the basis that it made the same sexual pleasures available to women—who, research showed, had the same sexual needs and desires—that had long been available to men.

Second, both the classical world and the sexual revolution approached sexual ethics as chiefly a question of how an individual person's sexual behavior related to the life of the city. The main difference is that the sexual revolution came after the advent of whiteness and all that followed and was thus deeply conditioned by those assumptions. For example, the sexual revolution came after the rise of the idea that it was right and good for people to be able to create their own identities, regardless of how that affects neighbor or nature.

We might put it this way: In the Roman world, the stability of the city was uncertain, so the Romans cared very much that the limitless sexual energies of powerful men be contained. If they were not, the life of the city could be irrevocably damaged. In the post-sexual revolution world, the roles have been reversed, but much of the underlying logic is similar, particularly the way in which sex is used to help stabilize a desired good that is perceived to be uncertain or unstable. What is uncertain today is the individual self. To be one's authentic self is an enormous challenge because so many forces in society fight against authenticity. The state, meanwhile, is relatively stable, built on unfathomable amounts of wealth and remarkably powerful social institutions, especially big business and big government.

So the question in our day is how these large entities can help people direct their sexual energies in ways that allow them to be their true, authentic selves. The movement begins with what is stable, and it uses sex to bring stability to the unstable. Both the classical world and the sexual revolution share the assumption that sexual energy is uncontainable, that sex is essential to the good life, and that the proper way of thinking about sexual behavior is to judge it by whether or not it strengthens an unstable, uncertain social body—the city in the classical world, and the individual self in the modern world.

THE WORLD THE SEXUAL REVOLUTION HAS MADE

What kind of world did the sexual revolution create? Several themes quickly became apparent.

First, though it rhymes with the classical world at many points, the sexual revolution foregrounds consent in a way the ancient world never did. This makes sense, of course, because so much of the revolutionary society is wrapped up in ideas of advancing personal liberty. Yet what the sexual revolution attempts to do is striking: it wants to reassert the broadly permissive sexual practices of the pre-Christian world while retaining the centrality of consent in sexual ethics. Thus the sexual revolution is far more egalitarian than classical society.

But where did the idea of consent as central to licit sexuality come from in the first place? The answer is Christianity. It was St. Paul, after all, who said that within marriage the husband's body belongs to his wife—a shocking and even scandalous idea to the Roman world. Thus the sexual revolution has tried to retain elements of Christianity while dramatically expanding sexual possibilities.

But this doesn't altogether work. Consent works better within covenants than hookups, as the Presbyterian Church in America's committee report on human sexuality put it.[11] Because of this, our society has had to stretch the idea of consent. It's not hard, for example, to see that internet pornography fulfills a similar role in our society that the slave class did in the Roman world: it's an outlet for our society's pent-up sexual energy. This is justified on grounds that sex workers have consented to have sex on camera and to have the video distributed for mass consumption ("consumption" being perhaps even more descriptive than many would like to admit).

However, all "consent" means in this case is that a person has signed a contract saying they agree to x in exchange for payment y.

That's a very thin conception of consent. Under what circumstances did the sex worker first consent to participate in pornographic films? Under what circumstances have they continued to consent to do so? If your argument considers only the signed contract and ignores the rampant financial needs that often drive people to sex work—as well as the epidemic of drug abuse and addiction common among sex workers, and the very real problem of sex trafficking endemic in the porn industry—then your conception of consent is deeply capitalistic and prone to the same abuses that we have already seen in industrialism, which privileged financial claims over social, cultural, or spiritual concerns.

This is all too predictable. Maintaining a clear doctrine of consent in a culture that begins with assumptions of isolation, detachment, and homelessness is enormously difficult. A rich conception of consent is difficult in a world where the assumed natural state is violence, the natural state of the human person is detached autonomy, and the purpose of human life is to project the authentic self into the world. None of these beliefs align well with a robust vision of consent, which is premised on the idea of suppressing one's own needs and desires to accommodate the preferences of one's neighbor. We might say that in this vision of reality, and of sexuality in particular, consent is less about preserving the ongoing conditions of love and self-giving and more about protecting against the worst excesses of revolutionary society. Thus the concept of consent is always imperiled, always being negotiated and defined. This is not a stable foundation for healthy sexual relationships.

This brittle conception of consent leads to a second problem with sexuality after the sexual revolution. There's a story in the popular imagination that sees the 1960s as the era when all the sexual energies long suppressed by Christian strictures were unleashed, leading to a blossoming of human freedom, possibility, and individuality. Finally the chains of Christianity had been cast off.

But this account badly misrepresents the world prior to the 1960s. Many of the underlying habits of mind, values, and concerns that led to the sexual revolution were already in place in the Western world for some time prior to the sexual revolution. As far back as the sixteenth century, whiteness had been used to justify an unimaginably cruel degree of socialized selfishness, which privileged the European desire to self-designate at the expense of virtually all Indigenous life in the Americas. The history that follows the advent of whiteness is largely a history of expanding whiteness into new domains and affording new peoples the same access to self-designation that was enjoyed by the Spanish conquistadores and their national leaders during the conquest of the Americas.

The right way of understanding the sexual revolution is not as the triumph of human freedom over the controlling and inhuman moralizing of Christianity. Instead, it was a further step in securing the rights of each person to self-designate over and against the Christian vision—a Christian vision which, at its best, provided a safe context for sexual relationships while also providing an account of human flourishing that did not require any sexual experience at all. What citizens of the classical world learned, and what I expect many will discover in the years to come, is that the Christian account of sexuality is both more restrictive *and* more humane than the hedonistic account currently in favor.

Viewed this way, the danger of the sexual revolution becomes more apparent. In the Christian conception of sexuality, the self's identity is secured ultimately in Christ but also proximally in the covenant of marriage. This securing of the self makes it possible to view sex as chiefly an act of self-giving rather than self-realization. It reorients the sexual act away from our own needs, experiences, and desires and toward the needs, experiences, and desires of the other. It is able to do this because sex is ultimately unnecessary as a way of defining our identity. Sex is not necessary to live a good life.

All the pressures that come with sex when it is seen as a primary way to self-designate are removed in the Christian vision of sexuality. A person can see their sexual life as being chiefly about serving and loving their partner. Tim Keller explains it well:

> In Ancient Rome there was usually one party—the party with power—using the other party as an object to satisfy his physical

needs. Today often the parties are both using one another, treating the other party as an object to meet needs, to be related to only as long as those needs are being met. . . . Christian theology answers that sex . . . must image God and in particular his redeeming love. Sex is not about enhancing one's power but about mutually giving up power to one another in love, as Christ did for us.[12]

In the sexual revolution's account of human sexuality, an act that ought to seal the bond between covenanted partners is instead chiefly an act of self-expression, a means of projecting our true self into the world. Thus our sexual partner is reduced from "the beloved" and transformed into an accessory for our own sexual expression.

Finally, the sexual revolution raises major questions concerning the necessity of sex. One consequence of making sex a primary way to project our identities is that it raises difficult questions about the "right to sex." Followed to their natural conclusion, these questions lead to some alarming conclusions, as Ross Douthat noted in a 2018 column about the rising number of "involuntary celibates," or "incels" in the contemporary West.[13]

If satisfying sexual experiences are required to live an authentically good life, then a "right to sex" naturally follows. That leaves us with two political possibilities. First, consent could be further weakened in the cases of people who are unable to attract a sexual partner yet are still guaranteed a right to sex. Alternatively, society could regard on-demand pornography and on-demand sex dolls as a kind of de facto human right for those who are unable or unwilling to seek out human sexual partners.

But this simply reprises the problem mentioned above: How do we understand the consent that sex workers give to pornographers and their audiences? What do we make of the fact that drug and alcohol abuse, as well as income insecurity, are endemic among sex workers, suggesting that sex workers are consenting under duress? Our egalitarian society is more like the Roman world than we care to admit. We simply have, in typical modern fashion, displaced the suffering that our worldview creates. The colonialists displaced suffering by exporting it to the Americas and later to Africa and parts of Asia. Today, we outsource it to sex workers and impoverished factory workers all over the Majority World.

In this sense we may actually be worse than the classical world. For the Roman world, the suffering of the slave population had to be rationalized, but for us the suffering of our de facto slave population can be ignored, suppressed by the distance and lack of personal contact afforded to us by our technology. There are alternatives to such a world, of course, but they involve a far more radical rethinking of what healthy sex actually is. To raise such questions is to attack not only the sexual revolution but also our revolutionary society writ large, and this is precisely what revolutionaries are never willing to do.

And so, as with the industrial revolution, the answer to the crisis brought about by the sexual revolution is to press deeper into the logic of the revolution, as we will see in the next chapter.

5

THE UNMAKING
OF THE REAL

Wonder Among the Institutions

The Monty Python movie *The Meaning of Life* begins with a scene called "The Miracle of Birth." In it, a pregnant woman in labor is carted through sterile gray halls on a stretcher, slammed noisily through swinging doors with a bang and a wince every few seconds before she is brought to the delivery room.

Before she is wheeled in, the camera cuts to the doctors, who enter the spartan room and remark that it seems a bit empty. They promptly ask their assistants to cart in an array of machines, including the most expensive one, "in case the administrator arrives," and "the machine that goes 'ping!'"—which, we later learn, tells doctors that "the baby is alive."

From here absurdity piles on absurdity: Once all the machines have been set up, the two doctors, played by John Cleese and Graham Chapman, remark that there is still something missing. They have all the machines as well as a full complement of nurses. Suddenly they look at each other and at the same time realize their mistake: the patient is missing. They then begin calling out, "Patient! Patient!" as one might call a pet. Then one of the nurses discovers the patient laid out on a stretcher and tucked away behind several other machines.

They move her to the operating table, and a number of observers are brought into the room. One man in front begins speaking to the patient, and the doctors ask who he is. "The husband," he replies. The doctors order him out of the room, explaining that "only people involved are allowed in here." So the husband is ushered out while his wife is left with a staff of doctors, nurses, a number of donors, and, finally, the administrator himself, who turns up just as the husband is being removed from the room.

The administrator exchanges pleasantries with the staff, remarking on all the machines before asking the staff what they are working on today. "A birth," the doctors say, further explaining that a birth is "when we take a new baby out of a lady's tummy." The administrator replies, "Ah, wonderful things we can do nowadays!"

The woman gives birth. One doctor uses a cleaver to cut the cord and the other shows the baby to the mother. Then they "sedate her, number the child, measure it, blood type it, and . . . isolate it!" A nurse announces, "Show's over!" and everyone exits the room. The doctors speak briefly with the mother, who asks the baby's gender, to which the doctor played by Chapman replies, "I think it's a bit early to be imposing roles, don't you?" The doctors exit the room, leaving the woman alone, with only the machines for companions. "Ping!" goes the machine, and the scene ends.[1]

THE LOSS OF THE REAL

One way to understand the crisis of our day is as a kind of slowly growing sense of deprival. It is a story of how more and more elements of the humane life are obscured by social transformations and institutions that have inserted themselves between our lives and reality. Thus the humor in the Monty Python sketch: There are few things more wondrous than the birth of a child. And yet well-intentioned and often necessary medical care has come over time to obstruct the essential experience of birth that defines a child's first entry into the world. And birth, of course, is not the only place this happens.

In the first chapter, I argued for the importance of a thick conception of nature. Contrary to the claims of many of our peers (as well as many historic figures—go read Homer), the world is not primordially violent and chaotic. Rather, the world is the fruit of God's intentional action. We did not arrive in this world by accident. The world itself is not an accident. The places we live are not the aftermath of a sort of cosmic car crash but are designed by God to promote human and creaturely flourishing. Nature, as understood by historic Christianity, is a coherent thing, an order, a plan of love and truth.

Before we put our kids to bed at night, I pray this prayer with them from the Book of Common Prayer: "Lighten our darkness, we beseech thee, O Lord; and by thy great mercy defend us from all perils and dangers of this night; for the love of thy only Son, our Savior, Jesus Christ. Amen."[2] It's an old prayer, but something important is happening in it. It's the prayer we pray as evening falls, as we close our eyes and rest our heads on the pillow. It is, in other words, a prayer we use before entering our most vulnerable state. When we sleep, we are unable to act to protect ourselves. When we sleep, we're entrusting our safety to something else—the locks on our doors, customs and norms that run against burglarizing houses, and the threat of legal recriminations should anyone attack us in our sleep. Yet all these protections can fail. Houses are broken into, after all. What's more, natural disaster can strike—a storm can blow over a tree, which can fall into our living room. A faulty bit of wiring in the kitchen can cause a fire. For all our efforts, our safety during this time of vulnerability is not guaranteed. And so we pray, asking God to protect us in the night.

It's possible to be vulnerable and yet still safe. This simple evening prayer teaches us one of the most important things we can learn in this world. Though the world is often violent and dangerous, we need not give ourselves over to a spirit of fear. We can still, in one sense, be at home in the world. Because of this, it is possible for us to recognize our own vulnerability to the world's evils without feeling the need to escape from the world or subdue it to our mastery.

Over the course of the modern era, beginning in colonialism, this experience of being vulnerable and yet still belonging in the world has been eroded. Our capacity to feel at home in the world has been eroded as more and more of created reality is estranged from us. In chapter two's description of the colonial move, we saw that one important aspect of the founding of modernity was the divorcing of the human person and their identity from the natural landscapes, the rhythms and seasons of their home, their culture, and their neighbors. Colonialism eroded all of this by transforming everything outside of my body into a "thing," to use Simone Weil's term.

The industrial revolution pressed further into this trend, wantonly violating nature for the sake of material gain and divorcing human beings from any sense of ownership or meaning in their work. The sexual revolution pressed still further into these realities by observing the "emancipation" that men had received via employed work outside the home and that children received via mandatory schooling, and by deeming that the only fair thing to do was to likewise emancipate women from the home, launching them into the same world of alienated work that men had been shot into a century before. If industrialism broke the productive household, the sexual revolution broke the natural family.

All these losses have been significant. And yet now we turn to something even more basic: the move to deprive humanity of a sense of wonder as they encounter God's world.

WHAT DO WE MEAN BY WONDER?

I grew up in an old railroad town that had long before been annexed by the city of Lincoln, Nebraska, but most of my friends lived "out in the country," as we described it. One lived on a farm outside Seward, a small town a half hour west of Lincoln, which was too far to be practical for play dates. But two other friends lived on acreages on the outskirts of Lincoln. These acreages became the sites of some of my most important childhood memories.

There was a creek out behind one friend's house, bounded on both sides by a thin line of trees. We would jump over the creek, explore it for rocks and small animals, and sometimes build small ramshackle structures in the woods. This friend also had a trampoline—

and not one of today's trampolines with a protective net to keep us from falling off. Their trampoline was completely open. This, of course, meant that our wrestling matches on it came with a certain risk—if you didn't watch your step, you could slip and fall off. One time my best friend and I convinced his little brother, who was probably in first or second grade at the time, to bounce on the trampoline while we launched water balloons at him from about fifty yards away. I had brought a water balloon launcher with me—essentially a giant rubber band with a pocket sown into it to hold the water balloons—and we decided to have some fun at his brother's expense. After the first few went flying past him at high speed—a good launcher can shoot the balloons at nearly a hundred miles an hour—he ran inside, and we were spared the trouble we would have been in had we actually hit him.

My other friend also had a trampoline. His was set up near a large outdoor play fort his dad had made for him and his brother. Crucially, the fort included a rope swing. And so we created a game in which we attempted to use the rope to swing from the fort to the trampoline, jumping off the swing at its highest point and trying to make it all the way to the trampoline. (That we did all these things without ever breaking a bone is, you'll probably agree, one of the world's great mysteries.) This friend's home was also the site for late-night games of Ghost in the Graveyard. Our version of the game, which I've also heard called "Ghosty Ghosty," involved identifying two bases. For us, the bases were often the propane tank, which was about twenty yards past his house, and the old barn on the opposite side of the property. One person, the ghost, would hide somewhere between the two bases. The remaining players would count while the ghost hid. Then they would try to run from one base to the other without being tagged.

It was not an altogether safe game. One time, a friend was running at full speed trying to escape the ghost when he ran directly into a clothesline strung between two poles. Unfortunately for him, his forehead was the same height as the clothesline. The line bent slightly as he ran into it and then snapped back, instantly knocking him off his feet and leaving an ugly welt across his forehead. It only took a few hours before we all thought the whole thing was hilarious. After all, how many people can say they've been clotheslined by an actual clothesline?

These places, these games, and these people are some of the dominant images of my childhood. They are how I first encountered the world and began to make sense of it. They are the people I grew up with. I sometimes worry that when we talk about feeling a sense of wonder in the world, we sound like we're describing some remarkable experience in which we're caught up into some ecstatic moment of contemplation. To be sure, these experiences do happen and can be significant and good. But to talk about wonder only in those terms can do it a disservice, as if it's only accessible to people with a certain imaginative capacity or a more sentimental spirit. When I talk about wonder, I mean something like the experiences my friends and I shared growing up, constantly being thrust out of doors (and away from video games) by our parents (bless them) and into the wild, or at least something approximating "the wild."

The wonder I have in mind is the million imperceptible instances of youth when we find that the world is strange and interesting, and somehow feels right to us. It's that moment when a rock is propped up, revealing a swarm of insects and bugs crawling underneath and fleeing deeper into the dirt as we boys quickly dig even deeper, trying to catch them. It's that thrill we feel as the air rushes over our face as we leap over a creek. It's that surge of adrenaline we feel as we're slowly walking through a dark field at night and suddenly hear a friend shout out "ghost in the graveyard!" and we sprint with abandon toward the barn, feeling the grass brush against our feet and the air surge past our body—hopefully without hitting a clothesline.

These experiences expanded our imaginations, which is to say they enlarged our idea of what the world was, what we could do in it, and the pleasure it could give us. They instilled in us the idea that we could be surprised by the world without being threatened by it, by taking the time to know this world was something worthwhile and rewarding. It taught us, as Marilynne Robinson put it, that "this is an interesting planet. It deserves all the attention you can give it."

One of my favorite pictures of my oldest son shows him, then four years old, sitting in our backyard, slouching down in a kid-size lawn chair, legs stretched as far as they'll go, overlarge rain boots on his feet, sucking on a popsicle. It's an image of youth, someone who is only beginning to discover the world and yet who already has found ways of being comfortable in it—who has found that it is good.

THE DEPRIVAL OF WONDER

In his book *Deschooling Society* the Czech tech critic Ivan Illich argues that much of our experience of the world today is obstructed and conditioned by institutions. He refers to this as the institutionalization of values. Illich was particularly concerned with education. Writing in the 1970s, he argued that schools have transformed something as expansive and central to human experience as learning into a kind of mechanical process.

What *should* learning be? According to Illich, learning is what happens when we open our eyes to the world and begin to make sense of it. We hear the bird's song and then learn to name it: cardinal, mourning dove, blue jay. We see something gently falling from the sky and then learn its name—snow—and begin to play in it. Education helps us to open our eyes to the world with greater knowledge, which in turn helps us to respond to the world with greater care, to interact with it in ways that tend toward health and flourishing. "Nothing in the intellect that is not first in sense," said the Catholic educator John Senior. Senior also said that wonder is our birthright as human beings and, following the lead of Aristotle, that wonder must come before wisdom. Before we can learn to act responsibly and wisely in the world, we must be astonished by it. Of course, this sort of education is obtained by simply living, as another educator, the nineteenth-century British theorist Charlotte Mason, well knew. "Education is an atmosphere . . . a life," Mason said. Education happens all around us and all the time simply because we are humans and the world is interesting and able to speak to us. I see my father working on the car and I go stand next to him to see what he is doing. I see a friend's sibling feeding the chickens and I watch. I hear my mother playing the piano and I go to watch as she presses the pedals, her fingers dancing across the keys as the sound of "Für Elise" fills the home.

But this, Illich argues, is not the sort of education offered in most schools. Instead, our schools offer education from textbooks and according to expert-approved curricula. And so we are taught two things before we are even old enough to realize that we *are* being taught. First, we are told that learning is something that only happens when we are interacting with approved authorities within the confines of an approved institution. Learning happens when I open the textbook and read the assigned pages. It does not happen when I am out at recess, watching a robin hop on a branch. Second, learning is something we consume via the designated authorities, not something we actively pursue ourselves as part of our birthright as human beings bearing the divine image.

Our education systems condition us to regard our lives as a movement from institution to institution, to experience reality only as it is mediated to us by the appropriate authorities. The wild-eyed thrill of a boy rushing through the woods, leaping over creeks, and thrusting his hands into the dirt is not condemned or opposed so much as it is implicitly eliminated as a possibility from the start. Indeed, because the household and the family are both in decline, most young children today enter institutional life as babies and never have the chance to simply encounter the world unmediated by adults or institutions. From an early age we learn to interpret the world with the aid of institutions, and we learn that life is chiefly a matter of consumption rather than making.

To be clear, the issue here is not that institutions are inherently bad in themselves. Rather, the issue is that many institutions have become the chief means by which the divide between people and the world is maintained and even reinforced. Illich uses the idea of "iatrogenesis" to explain the problem. Originally, iatrogenesis referred to medical problems caused by doctors or nurses attempting to cure a patient. In contemporary terms, the all-too-common story of a person being severely injured and then becoming addicted to painkillers during their treatment could be seen as an example of iatrogenesis. Likewise, in society, iatrogenesis occurs when an institution that is meant to promote some desired good comes to do greater harm in the pursuit of that good. How does this happen? Illich uses the example of two "watershed" moments in medical care to explain it.

The first watershed comes when a new technology emerges and produces a rapid and significant improvement in quality of life. This happened in the first half of the twentieth century in American medical care as vaccines eradicated once-devastating diseases and the discovery of penicillin made it possible to treat many common illnesses more effectively. But then a second watershed comes when the original goal is lost and the technology or institution becomes self-referential, judged only by how well it serves its own ends. Illich explains it in *The Convivial Society*, arguing that a "second watershed" has been reached when new technologies and techniques are adopted not because they substantially improve human lives but because they serve the needs of an institution.[3]

In other words, once we pass Illich's second watershed, an institution is no longer judged by whether it serves society in some real, tangible way in keeping with its original intent. Rather, it is judged by standards it has defined for itself. We can see a similar process in the economy: The American economy was, in one sense, booming throughout the 1980s and 1990s. But the boom didn't necessarily mean higher wages for average American workers or an improvement in the quality of American life as good work was done in service of neighbor. All that a "booming economy" meant was that the stock market was healthy and people who had invested in stocks were doing well for themselves. The actual relationship between the economic growth of that era and the status of ordinary American workers was tenuous at best.

Likewise, we can see the process of iatrogenesis in the American education system. Students in America will receive a standardized curriculum and a standardized reading list (consisting almost entirely of textbooks). We are taught that the purpose of our education is to equip us to pass standardized tests before passing into an adulthood of standardized work in the capitalist marketplace. The school becomes a preparatory lab for contemporary capitalism, a factory that contains children until they're able to be productive. And so educational institutions are no longer evaluated according to whether their students graduate with a love of learning, a delight in the world, or a desire to cultivate their minds. They are, rather, judged by test scores, graduation rates, and, for colleges, job placement rates.

If we compare it to the model of education described above, we might say that most schooling—and the Christian school I attended as a young person was actually worse about this than every public school I have encountered—does not begin with a child opening their eyes to reality but rather with the curriculum makers packing reality into boxes, which are shipped and opened by the students in their approved desks in their approved classrooms under the approved supervision of credentialed professionals.

And so we encounter only the parts of the world that can be made to fit into boxes, that can be transformed into standardized curriculum, that can be addressed on standardized tests. This deprival of wonder is both more basic and more horrifying than much of what we have already described.

THE DANGER OF A SINGLE STORY

In her talk, "The Danger of a Single Story," the Nigerian novelist Chimamanda Ngozi Adichie describes her childhood encounters with books and writing as a young girl living in eastern Nigeria. Though she had never been out of Nigeria, Adichie grew up reading American and British children's books. And, she explains, this shaped her imagination in ways that created a distance between herself and her home:

> When I began to write, at about the age of seven, stories in
> pencil with crayon illustrations that my poor mother was

obligated to read, I wrote exactly the kinds of stories I was reading: All my characters were white and blue-eyed, they played in the snow, they ate apples, and they talked a lot about the weather, how lovely it was that the sun had come out. Now, this despite the fact that I lived in Nigeria. I had never been outside Nigeria. We didn't have snow, we ate mangoes, and we never talked about the weather, because there was no need to. My characters also drank a lot of ginger beer, because the characters in the British books I read drank ginger beer. Never mind that I had no idea what ginger beer was.[4]

The single story Adichie received about little White children in Europe and America enjoying the food, drink, and weather of that place caused her to not really *see* her place. Curriculum makers and entertainment producers had essentially defined the world for Adichie before she was old enough to encounter it for herself and to take in reality in all its surprising wonder and distinct local forms.

This is the danger in a prepackaged education guided by curriculum and textbooks. Such an education has a way of imperceptibly placing itself between us and the world, which has the effect of both obscuring what's in front of us and teaching us to encounter reality chiefly through mediation, rather than through a direct encounter with the world. In his poem "How to Be a Poet," Wendell Berry counsels his readers to "breathe with unconditional breath the unconditioned air" and "stay away from anything that obscures the place it is in."[5] The poem might as well be called "How to Be a Person." What's most dangerous and pernicious about our society is the way it makes this sort of encounter with reality much rarer and more difficult.

HUMANITY IN EXILE

In chapter two, we considered the launch of Sputnik I as modernity at its zenith. When we flung that small metal ball into orbit, we were announcing to the universe and to ourselves that we could escape the confines of this planet, that we could reach for the stars and someday find that they are within our grasp. It was a romantic dream, but it has not turned out as those scientists first dreamed—as our emancipation from the confines of this planet, our home. It has turned out that sundering the ties that bind us to Mother Earth does not actually liberate us but condemns us to a deep loneliness, a sense of being unhooked from our places, our neighbors, and ourselves.

The Soviets launched the satellite from a research lab and launch base in southern Kazakhstan—a remote corner of the old Soviet empire that allowed for the kind of experimentation that the postwar Soviet Union wished to pursue. The remoteness of Kazakhstan offered other benefits that soon suggested themselves to Soviet leaders.

In addition to being an ideal site for scientific experimentation—which included nuclear testing as well as space exploration—it was also an excellent place to put political prisoners that could not, for whatever reason, simply be kept in the gulags of Siberia. And so while Soviet scientists were running the early experiments that would culminate in Sputnik I, the great Russian writer Alexander Solzhenitsyn, recently freed from a Siberian concentration camp but still deemed too dangerous to be allowed to return to civilian life, was living a hundred miles away from that lab in a remote village called Birlik. And so, within this small, hundred-mile area of an obscure corner of the old Soviet Union were both the hope of modernity, symbolized by Sputnik I, and perhaps modernity's most perceptive and trenchant critic, fresh from a stint in Stalin's gulags.

Eventually Solzhenitsyn would leave Kazakhstan. In time, he would be sent into exile in the West. Perhaps, you think, a writer like him would find "freedom" in the West. He would revel in the openness and even permissiveness that was unimaginable behind the Iron Curtain. But he did not. He found revolution in America too, indeed one surprisingly similar to the one he had so resisted in his native Russia. True, the Soviet Union was communist and America was capitalist. But this, to Solzhenitsyn, was not as important a difference as many thought. In a speech given at the Harvard University commencement in 1978, he told America about this revolution and explained why America, as it then existed, could not actually be the hope of the world—or even an authentic foil to the Soviet system.

Solzhenitsyn argued that the only source the West had found for guiding our moral lives is explicit statements in our legal codes. This is inevitable, of course, because of the way we imagine the human person. If the human person is naturally solitary and autonomous, then the only things to guide our behavior are our own ambitions and synthetically defined legal norms and laws that seek to prevent the worst excesses and abuses that come from people given over to their ambition. The reason our moral lives are guided by the letter of the law is because that is all the revolution of these past centuries has left us with once it has destroyed nature and rejected God. In our own day this problem has had sufficient time to work itself out, and we now find it difficult to distinguish between the legal and the moral, even the legal and the spiritual.

The effect has been the hollowing out of our spiritual lives, even the hollowing out of our humanity. What was left of America, Solzhenitsyn argued, was the husk of law. The inner life that the law was meant to protect had been eaten away by materialism and affluence. The law still existed, but it had fallen into iatrogenesis; it had become disconnected from actual questions of justice, goodness, and truth. It was now only self-referential. And this created many problems for communal life in America.

When a people's life together can only be governed by rules, it can only be directed to materialistic goals. Procedure knows nothing of love. Rigid and unyielding laws know nothing of human relationship. All procedure can do is guarantee external behaviors and external measures of wealth and success. Anyone who has grown up in a strict fundamentalist church can relate to this: as long as you adhere to the church's behavioral norms, your inner life can be utterly graceless and godless and no one will have the slightest idea. But eventually, such a life ceases to be sustainable. And that's when the collapse comes.

Our obsession with the material, Solzhenitsyn said, leaves the human soul atrophied and the natural world desolate. Solzhenitsyn looked at the West and saw a spiritual wasteland. True, he acknowledged, the West was free of the explicit forms of cruelty and tyranny that dominated his native and beloved Russia. But he did not see the West as a hope for Russia or anywhere else. What he saw was a spiritually emaciated society that disguised its sickness with "mechanical legalistic smoothness."[6] But this smoothness was only on the surface—and, he warned, the surface was alarmingly thin. Unless the West learned to look back to the old ways, to recognize the human creature's place within a transcendent order, then it too would wither. "The human soul longs for things higher, warmer, and purer than those offered by today's mass living habits, introduced by the revolting invasion of publicity, (and) TV stupor," he said. We can only imagine what this great soul of twentieth-century Russia would say if he could see Twitter and Instagram and twenty-four-hour news.

What did he propose as a way through the revolution? We must turn our eyes upward to the heavens, he said, not as a place to conquer, as his compatriots in the space program believed, but as a reminder that our lives exist as a vapor in the wind, and then comes the judgment.

We do not conquer the heavens; we are judged by them. And if we fail to discover the sources of spiritual health, there is nothing else for us. Our spiritual lives will continue to be trampled on by the weight of our age. And if our spiritual lives are destroyed, no amount of wealth or power can atone for such a loss.

6

AGAINST THE REVOLUTION

The Beginnings of Christian Social Doctrine

The problems began with Toogaboochu. That, at least, is what my roommate and I told ourselves as we spent day after day pulling up weeds in the woods that sat between the two L'Abri houses. L'Abri is a residential Christian study center where students can come for a time to work within the community and study topics of interest to them—it's not *quite* a Christian commune, but it certainly resembles one in many ways. Anyway, we were working together in the woods, pulling up a hateful weed called buckthorn, or *rhamnus cathartica* (the similarity to *cathartic* is a cruel joke). This invasive species can grow up to twenty feet tall and take over huge swathes of land if left unchecked—and at L'Abri it had been unchecked. Our tutor, Jock, sometimes worked with us, walking around in the woods in cheap, fluorescent, dollar store flip-flops, carrying a chainsaw with him and attacking the buckthorn with relish. Pity the fool whose job it was to follow behind him with the weed killer that we used to kill the stumps. (Reader, I was that fool.) The weed was originally from Europe and had made its way over to Minnesota as a popular hedging material. But, as often happens, the people who brought the weed didn't know what they were doing, and soon Minnesota had an epidemic of buckthorn, choking out the native plants and wildlife. And so it was in the small, wooded area between the L'Abri houses.

That's the story the Minnesotans tell, anyway. My roommate and I had a different story. The weed was so rampant, we thought it had to have some supplemental aid as it grew. Enter Toogaboochu. We imagined that there was a little forest demon named Toogaboochu that lived in Buckthorn Forest—our name for the woods between the houses. Every night, this small elfin creature snuck around the woods planting more buckthorn. He was deceptively quick and had a wicked sense of humor. We sometimes joked that we saw him through the trees at sunset, preparing for his night's work, taunting us from afar.

We hated Toogaboochu.

And every day we waged war against him, sometimes on our own, sometimes following Jock and his fluorescent flip-flops and chainsaw. Then one morning, a couple weeks into our campaign, we sat at the breakfast table and saw dark, heavy rain clouds roll in. Like little boys naively hoping that Dad would give them the day off, we both looked at Jock eagerly to see if he would cancel the day's buckthorn weeding. He smiled at us mischievously. (Jock and Toogaboochu shared a sense of humor.)

"You're not thinking about this the right way," he told us. "If the ground is wet, the weeds will come up even easier!" He slapped us on the back as we followed him outside. He set us to work and then, in true dad fashion, went inside to do some office work as the rain began to fall. A couple hours later we were chilled to the bone. But the buckthorn *had* come up easier. It was a good morning's work. A hot shower and lunch would feel good.

First, though, it being L'Abri, we went inside for tea. As we entered, we kicked off our shoes and took off our coats and walked through the kitchen into the living room. A fire was going in the wood-burning stove and the room was warm. A few other guests were already there, as were a couple of the permanent residents. Norah Jones's "Come Away with Me" was on the stereo. We sat down and were served warm mugs of tea in the only acceptable fashion at L'Abri—PG Tips, two teaspoons of sugar, and a splash of milk.

To this day, the sound of that record, the gentle crackling of a fire, and the taste of PG Tips all take me back to that room, those friends, that summer. The warmth and feeling of belonging that washes over me in memory is so comforting that it even makes me forgive Toogaboochu.

If Christianity has anything to say to the revolutionary society, the words must ultimately speak of something like that memory. If we are to have anything to say to our non-Christian neighbors, many of whom are increasingly likely to see Christians as vain hypocrites, then our words must ultimately be directions to places like that living room—not just for the comforts of tea time, delightful as those are, but also the work done against our fancied forest demon, work that was necessary for the health of the woods and the wildlife that called it home. They must be directions, in short, to beloved community gathered together around good work.

These days the buckthorn has been much reduced, and on my last visit to L'Abri I was greeted at the top of the drive by a family of deer that have since moved into Buckthorn Forest. All of this, the work and the pleasure, the humor and the labor, is part of Christian belonging. If we can't speak of Christian belonging and common life in ways that suggest something like this sort of life, then we ultimately have nothing to say to our neighbors.

Why is it that this vision of Christian belonging seems so remote and impossible today? We've already answered the question in part: The revolutionary vision of society, which shapes our world at so many levels, is itself hostile to belonging, making the possibility of a "home" less and less real. The invention of whiteness began with the assumption that neighbors and land could be reduced to objects that don't require certain kinds of responses from other people. Similarly, industrialism proceeded by breaking cultures and ways of living that allowed for stronger communal life and thicker forms of belonging, starting in the household. The sexual revolution doubled down on all of this, continuing the work of pulling apart things that belong together—in this case pulling apart the sexual embrace and fruitful, faithful covenantal love, reconfiguring sex as little more than an especially intense form of pleasure and, maybe, of relationship building. Ultimately this all builds to a climax in the collapse of wonder and the triumph of institutions as all our encounters with reality are filtered through the objectives and goals of institutions.

In all these ways, we have attacked what Jennings calls the "ontological density" of the world. Unsurprisingly, as a result the world has felt more and more foreign to us. Perhaps that is why we have found it so easy to abuse the world so egregiously over the past two hundred years. Much of our recent history in the West is a protracted attempt to replace the weight and significance of love, rootedness, and neighborly affection with self-creation, self-realization, and self-actualization.

By contrast, life in a community like L'Abri offers an arresting picture of what home can be. One element of this is the space L'Abri offers for people who need to face difficult questions or work through traumatic (or even merely difficult) life experiences. But the reason L'Abri can do this profound work is much simpler than that work itself. My memories of L'Abri are mostly the taste of tea, the sound of music, the crackling fire, and the presence of friends, all in a space that feels like what you imagine home ought to be—safe, informal, governed by love rather than a restless need to be doing something or making something of oneself.

At bottom, L'Abri is about extending the offer of hospitality. It is about making yourself available to your neighbor, which in their case means not only next-door neighbors but whomever God brings to their door. In this sense, the possibility of offering and receiving the gift of belonging is wrapped up in the simple willingness to offer yourself to others.

It is in this posture that we can see an alternative to the ideology of whiteness that has become so characteristic of much of Western life today—not only in how it informs racial issues but in many other areas of life as well. It is in this posture of receptive openness that we can see an alternative to the centered self, projecting meaning into the world.

Where the revolutionary spirit is defined by a kind of mindless, trampling activity, receptive hospitality is defined by an intelligent, charitable passivity, not in the sense of being inactive but in the sense of being open to receiving the needs of others. Where revolutionary people project meaning into the world—which, more often than not, means imposing one's desires *onto* the world—a Christian posture of welcome seeks to embody Harmut Rosa's concept of "resonance," as neighbors and places act on each other, both seeking a mean where their relationship becomes a blessing to both.

INSTRUCTIONS IN CHRISTIAN LOVE

Another word for this receptiveness is *love*, which, of course, is what Jesus calls us to in the Gospels. It is to love that all Christians are called—first, love of God and then love of neighbor. The sixteenth-century Reformer Martin Bucer is a helpful model here because of how deeply he was concerned with Christians living in accordance with God's call to love. He offers a striking picture of what a Christian witness can look like if disentangled from the revolutionary spirit that is so foundational to how many of us approach the world.

While Catholic conquistadores and theologians from Spain and Portugal were in the New World, Bucer was in his home city of Strasbourg doing something radically different. For the entirety of his nearly thirty years of ministry in the city, Bucer sought to create a Christian society defined by a pervasive commitment to the simple piety imparted to us by Christ when he summarized all of God's law as loving God and loving neighbor. Bucer thought that the affluence and self-regard of the late medieval church had caused the simplicity of Christian practice to be lost.

In this, Bucer was an heir to Erasmus of Rotterdam, a man he admired who had once satirized the late medieval church by imagining a pope dying and, upon finding the doors of heaven locked against him, going off to rally the army he had led while he was pope to assail heaven itself. Presented with a chance to repent, church

leaders instead doubled down on past mistakes. Such was the deca-
dence and decay of the late medieval church. (That ours is not the
first era with such a badly compromised church might be a source of
encouragement.) Christian Europe had, according to both Erasmus
and Bucer, become indifferent to the poor and to the ordinary practices of Christian virtue. It had heaped up a thousand different
practices and norms that preserved itself, but it had forgotten more
basic things, including the law of love. So Bucer sought to lead the
church in Strasbourg in practices defined by mutual giving and a
thick sense of belonging among Christians, all brought about by a
commitment to taking up what he called "the yoke of Christ."[1]

From the beginning to the end of his life, Bucer was obsessed
with the problem of how exactly Christians can give and receive
love. His first published book was called *Instructions in Christian
Love*, but a more literal translation of the original title would be
"That No One Should Live for Himself but for Others." Even the
title suggests the sharp difference between Bucer's vision and the
revolutionary vision. The revolutionary centers the self and reduces
other people to things. But Christian love, according to Bucer, is
defined by an emptying of the self in service to others, an act which
mimics the humility and love of Jesus as described by St. Paul in
his letter to the Philippians. It is worth taking the time to consider
Bucer's account of love in some detail for a couple reasons. First, it
is a striking counterproposal to set against the emergence of
whiteness, which was happening on the other side of the world in
the Americas even as Bucer pastored his church and raised his
family in Strasbourg. Second, it is helpful to follow the overall
thought of a mature Christian who is concerned with Christian
love in a pervasive and socially weighty way, as Bucer was.

Bucer's account of Christian love is not sentimentalism or a kind
of naive do-goodism, like a premodern take on paying it forward.
Instead, he grounds Christian love in his account of God's love
flowing into every arena of life—the land itself included, which is
significant if Bucer is to offer us an alternative vision of Christian
maturity to set against the vision of the revolutionary society.

Early on in his account of Christian love, Bucer directs our eyes toward the land, toward animals and the natural world. He considers how nature itself is defined by generosity—a far cry from the more brutal vision of nature many of us have known: "The sky moves and shines not for itself but for all other creatures. Likewise the earth produces not for itself but for all other related things. . . . All the plants and all the animals, by what they are, have, can and actually do, are directed toward usefulness and helpfulness to other creatures and especially to man."[2] Bucer recognizes that the world is marked by a divinely given order, defined by peaceableness, generosity, and love—and that human beings ought to enter into that order with the same delight as the plants and animals do. When we live according to the law of love, we are doing what is natural to us as human beings.

We are never more natural than when we love. Why does this sound so strange to us then? Why are our encounters with the world and with our neighbors so often defined by pain and strife? Why do we encounter the world as, in Rosa's words, "a point of aggression"? Bucer says this is because human selfishness reverses the natural order of things. When we choose to live for ourselves, to center ourselves, we set ourselves at odds not only with the natural order of the world but more importantly with the God who created that order.

> With the loss of the knowledge of God we have lost also the knowledge of creatures. As we no longer wish to live to serve God, his creatures were rightly taken away from our service. If we ignore the Creator, it is fair that we are deprived also of the created. We have followed Satan and despised God. Hence our whole mind has been perverted to the point that it can no longer be useful to anyone. It has rather become so universally harmful that we have deserved for ourselves eternal condemnation. Thus the whole creation, which should have been used only to the praise and glory of its creator and for the preservation and profit of men, has been disgraced, profaned, and depraved by our diabolic misuse and self-seeking.[3]

The selfishness of humanity and the suffering of the world are tied closely together. Bucer would not be surprised at all that several hundred years of revolutionary thinking have set us on a path that makes the earth itself less conducive to human life.

If the testimony of the world itself were all that we needed to understand love, we would have no need of Jesus or Scripture. But, of course, the curse of sin afflicts the world and clouds our vision. So Bucer then considers the question of how people who have encountered Jesus ought to live in contrast to the selfishness and abuse of creation and creatures that defines lost human beings. Here he gets practical and considers the particular needs of the human person and what forms of work allow us to better meet those needs when we encounter them in our neighbor.

First, he suggests that because humanity's greatest need is spiritual renewal and a reestablishing of our relationship to God, the highest form of neighborly love is to commend the gospel to others and call our neighbors to repentance. The proclamation of the gospel to our neighbors is the highest form of work we can do. This includes pastoral ministry but is not limited to it. Bucer was actually somewhat fearful of ministry in the church precisely because of how corrupt the church had become. Bucer believed that the ministry of evangelization and discipleship is for all Christians. Next to that, he said, the work of governance is highest, for government secures the peace of a community and helps it pursue its common good together.

After the church and the government, what forms of life are most conducive to neighborly love and peaceable living? Bucer helps us see the pervasiveness of the call to Christian love and how completely that call is at odds with the revolutionary vision that was being established in the Americas at the same time. "The most Christian professions . . . are agriculture, cattle raising, and the necessary occupations therewith connected. These professions are the most profitable to the neighbors and cause them the least trouble. Every man should encourage his child to enter these professions because children should be encouraged to enter the best profession, and the best profession is the one which brings most profit to neighbors."[4] Thus the land is central to Bucer's vision of Christian love. For him, the most Christian profession is caring for land and animals and raising food for our neighbors. Even in his idea of "Christian professions," Bucer's vision consists of an outward movement of the self away from one's private interests and toward the sustaining and flourishing of the life of the world. What profession, Bucer asks, could possibly be more Christian than one that provides food for others and cares for our common home? But he does not stop there:

> (Many) men wish their children to become businessmen always with the idea that they would become rich without working, against the commandment of God, and with the idea that they will seek their own profit while exploiting and ruining others, against the divine order and the whole Christian spirit. Encouraging youth to enter that road is leading them to eternal death, while the path to eternal life is only through keeping the divine commandments.[5]

Much Christian discipleship in American churches has been based on the assumption that whatever discipleship looks like, it *won't* look like something that disrupts America's business and financial life. Whatever discipleship looks like, it can't be something that disrupts a comfortable privatized existence full of personal amusements and hobbies. Whatever discipleship looks like, it can't be something that would cost us the personal peace and affluence that we assume is our birthright as Americans.

Bucer warns us against this and reminds us that all of life is ruled by God, and that everything we do, every task our job requires of us, is done before the face of God. If Christ's lordship proves disruptive to our culture, then what must give isn't the call to Christian discipleship, but our lifestyles and the norms of our culture. All these things must be changed to better align with the teachings of Jesus.

How can we adopt this lifestyle of mutuality and joyful, sacrificial love? Bucer answers that question in the second half of his treatise. We do this, he says, through faith: "(People must) believe in Christ, fully trust that by His blood Christ has placed them again in the sonship and grace of the Father and that consequently by his Spirit Christ has also remade them according to the earliest world order, that is, useful to many and understanding all creatures."[6]

For Bucer, faith is synonymous with the assurance of being loved, and that assurance is synonymous with being compelled to give love to others. Bucer understood that our ability to give love depends on whether or not we have received love. And through the gospel, we know that we *have* received love, and thus the life of love is made available to us. Bucer's vision of Christian discipleship is founded in a sober recognition of our own frailty and inability to give love apart from the offer of help from outside ourselves. Our condition, so afflicted are we by sin, has become desperate, and it is only faith that can save us. Another German Christian, the twentieth-century martyr Sophie Scholl, describes this reality well in a letter she wrote to a close friend days before her martyrdom: "We're poor, weak, sinful children . . . However many little devils scurry around inside of me, I shall cling to the rope God has thrown me in Jesus Christ, even if my numb hands can no longer feel it."[7]

Thus Bucer ultimately calls us back to the vision we have already seen in chapter one: the resources needed for a life of love are themselves drawn from the eternal and unchanging love of God—the joy that he takes in existence itself and the invitation he extends to creation to share in that joy. In all these things, the vision of Christian common life and belonging offered to us in Bucer's treatise is the antithesis of the revolutionary society and, sadly, of many expressions of Christianity in the United States, which have sought to baptize the very sort of exploitative beliefs and practices that Bucer condemns so stridently, and which reverse the rightful ways life and goods are meant to move in God's world.

As we conclude our reading of Bucer, however, we confront a problem. The communities and rituals that Bucer saw as central to the exchanging of Christian love have not sat idly in a sealed, se-cured box that we can pick up, open, and experience for ourselves, unsullied and unchanged. The world has moved on since Bucer, and we now find ourselves on the other side of the revolutionary changes that Bucer's vision for life might have helped to prevent from ever happening.

Unfortunately, Bucer's particular project failed within his own lifetime. In 1549 the city of Strasbourg, Bucer's home since 1523, reverted to Catholicism as part of a peace treaty at the end of the First Schmalkaldic War. Bucer was banished from his home and eventually settled in England. He lived two years there, mostly unhappily, as he was separated from his wife and family for much of the time, since they stayed behind in Germany for a while after his departure. He deeply disliked both English food and English weather. He would die in 1551 with little work to show for the ministry of his final years and knowing that the work of his life in Strasbourg was already being undone. Six years later, Queen Mary would have his remains dug up and burned, scattering his ashes in the River Thames. Thus Bucer's legacy would be muted and suppressed even while his children were still alive. There is no Bucerian world for us to enter today.

It's all well and good, then, to learn from Bucer's example, especially since it was being articulated at the same time that whiteness was being invented in the Americas. Yet we cannot simply adopt it for ourselves due to the enormous distance that time has opened up between our world and his. True, we can learn from his example, but Bucer was living in a world that was already Christian in some ways. We, mostly, are not. So we cannot simply reappropriate a lost past through a withdrawal from the modern world. The revolutionary era we find ourselves in can only be lived through. But how do we do that? To answer that question we must consider the work and thought of other Christians who lived long after Bucer.

ORTHODOX YET MODERN

By the early 1900s, much of the transformative work of modernity was done. Political reform had swept across Europe, for good and for ill. Our relationship to the land and our work had been irrevocably changed by both colonialism and industrialism. This had, in turn, transformed the household, which in time would transform our relationship to sexuality, to our bodies, and to the family. All of this was already, even a hundred years ago, beginning to wreak havoc on common life. As we have already seen, the Dutch Calvinist Herman Bavinck summarized the problem neatly, saying that, "What strikes us in the modern age is the internal discord that consumes the self and the restless haste that drives it. . . . There is a disharmony between our thinking and feeling, between our willing and acting. There is a discord between religion and culture, between science and life."[8] It's a remarkably prescient comment for a book written in the early 1900s. The question facing the Western church, then, is what we would do in such a world. We ask now the same question our fathers and mothers in the faith asked in their day: "How can we sing the Lord's song in a foreign land?" Or, as Jennings puts it, "Who will we be in this strange new place?"

In his book *To Change the World*, sociologist James Davison Hunter suggests that there are ultimately four postures Christians have taken in response to the changes brought about by modernism: defensive against, relevance to, purity from, and faithful presence.[9] The first posture, "defensive against," is a generally conservative posture, favored in recent years by Christians who view the modern world as inextricably threatening to Christian faithfulness, so that the only posture we can take is to defend Christianity against the barbarism of modern life. This posture is largely what justified support for former President Trump during both the 2016 and 2020 elections. It is the posture of the culture warriors and the religious right. Significantly, this response to modernity is deeply modern in itself. The world that the defenders wish to preserve is nearly always the world that existed only a generation or two ago. And as any recent observer of the news well knows, White conservative Christians are among the most likely people to respond with indifference to racial injustice and, at times, to even support the institutions and norms that harm people of color.

This response, then, is both insufficient to the task before us and is compromised by a failure to reckon with the sources of our modern malaise, which is not moral relativism, or postmodernism, or critical race theory, to cite only three of the recent boogeymen so feared by the culture warriors. Our society's indifference to family and faith is grounded in an older indifference to geography and place, an indifference that, in fact, has its roots in Western racism.

A posture of "relevance to" is the progressive parallel adopted by many on the Christian left, such as Lutheran pastor Nadia Bolz-Weber. For these Christians, the nature of the relationship between Christianity and modernity is not so much Christianity against modernity, but Christianity flavoring modernity. Porn is bad but, to borrow a concept from Bolz-Weber, have you tried ethically sourced porn?[10]

Christianity is viewed as one religious system among many with truths to offer us as we seek to live better. But it would be wrong to absolutize its claims, as if the claims of Christian revelation should trump the claims of other belief systems or religions. For "relevance to" Christians, the story of Christianity and modernity is one of trying to discern how Christianity can make modern people better. But it has little capacity for critiquing modernity on its own terms.

Against both of these Hunter describes the posture favored by radical Anabaptists, which he labels "purity from." The "purity from" school is represented most famously by Stanley Hauerwas but has many adherents today, including activist Shane Claiborne and radical Anabaptist communities such as the Bruderhof.

For these Christians, there is a decisive conflict between Christianity and modernity, but the chief danger is not so much that modernity is directly antagonistic to the faith but that modernity tends to be corrosive to Christian fidelity over time. What concerns the "purity from" Christians is less the classic culture-war problems of prayer in school or sexual progressivism but more the ways modernity is, in fact, quite comfortable, even seductive, and can easily call us away from the life of serious Christian discipleship.

The failures of each of these three responses manifest in different ways. "Defensive against" Christians and "relevant to" Christians alike struggle to create genuinely alternative Christian communities because both have become so pervasively modern themselves, in different ways, that they aren't able to challenge modernity's cardinal sins. The "purity from" Christians, meanwhile, often provide us with a far more pervasive critique of our era's failings, yet because they live outside of that era in many ways, they effectively make Christian ideas and practices less accessible to the masses because most people will never have regular access to a Christian community such as the Bruderhof.

Ultimately, what's interesting about these failures is that they share a common root. All are insufficiently catholic—or "universal." Bavinck suggests that one way in which the Christian church is catholic is that it "embraces the whole of human experience."[11] A Christian witness that baptizes modernity, whether conservative or liberal, or that wholesale withdraws from it is, in this account, a failure of catholicity because each approach is failing to address all areas of life according to the truths revealed in Christian revelation. In describing catholic Christianity this way, Bavinck is working from the older thought of the fourth-century church father Cyril of Jerusalem, who wrote that "(the church) is called Catholic also because it brings into religious obedience every sort of man, rulers and ruled, learned and simple."[12] This is not a common application of the idea of catholicity, but it is one with roots in church history that we would do well to return to. This understanding of catholicity points us toward Hunter's fourth proposed response for how Christians ought to encounter the modern world: "faithful presence."

FAITHFUL PRESENCE IN PRACTICE

Faithful presence rejects each of the three prior visions. It sees Christian communities as always having robust internal practices wed to an evangelistic energy that is always radiating outward. A friend once observed that American Christians know what to do

when they have power and what to do when they do not have power.
What we don't know is how to *share* power. The response of faithful
presence seeks to provide such a vision.

By its very nature, faithful presence rules out certain things. It
rules out the reactionary posture of the culture warriors, who are
often simply warring against trends that are a generation further
down the modern drain than they themselves are. They consistently fail to put forward Christian alternatives to our world's vision
of constant acceleration. But faithful presence also does not mean
a capitulation to modernism, contrary to the "relevant to" Christians, who present Christianity as a kind of additive to help tamp
down modernity's worst excesses. Faithful presence does not mean
compromise; it does not mean accommodating wickedness. Faithful
presence means *actual presence*. We cannot withdraw from society
to preserve the purity of our faith. We live in neighborhoods and
work in institutions alongside non-Christian peers. We participate
in the lives of our cities and states and nations. To be sure, we do
all of this as Christians—and there may come a time when we are
not welcome. I myself have been fired from a freelance job because
of my Christian beliefs.

But there's a sharp difference between being cast out of a community one is willing to be part of and choosing to withdraw pre-
emptively. The latter forecloses the possibility of persuasion, of
transformation, of renewal. The former, in contrast, accepts the
possibility of loss, conflict, and strife as inherent in the call to
follow Jesus. And yet always it remains hopeful that unexpected
resurrection is possible, that God remains at work, and that God
calls his people to live among their neighbors, in the midst of their
city, and to labor for its good and even its glory.

7

THE EARTH IS OUR MOTHER

On Christianity, Land, and Animals

In 2007 Johannes Meier—a farmer and member of the Danthonia Bruderhof community in New South Wales, Australia—watched with dismay as a small creek that ran through the community's property dried up. Meier described the scene in an interview about the community's agricultural work, describing pools of water glutted with algae, filled with dead fish. There was no water flow at all. The stream was dry. Two years later, the creek dried up again. But something odd happened this time: when the creek bed was exposed, there were no fish to be found. This was when Meier knew something needed to be done. And so they began the work of figuring out where they'd gone wrong.

The answer will not be terribly surprising if you've followed our argument to this point: the trouble had begun with the farming practices of the White Europeans who had settled in Australia in the nineteenth century. Because much of Australia is naturally drier than Europe, plants had developed there that were adept at storing large amounts of water, which proved useful when drought hit, and water was at a premium. The reeds filling the Australian floodplains could be up to twelve feet tall, and the floodplains themselves could be as large as twenty-five miles across. To the Europeans, this all looked like unproductive swampland that needed to be drained to make room for grazing animals and monoculture farming. And so that's what they did. Soon, the landscape began to shift as the water that had been retained by these floodplains and sustained the land during dry seasons was now gone. Meier explains:

> In less than ten generations, Australia has seen massive erosion and desertification brought on by the destruction of functioning riparian areas and by farming practices that disregard the landscape's natural ability to hold water and keep salts at bay. Today, we're farming on subsoil, not topsoil. Natural plant and animal diversity is a shadow of what it was. With few plants to help store water in the landscape, slow its movement, spread fertility across flood plains, and control salts, when rainfall comes it washes out to sea, carrying with it untold tons of precious topsoil.[1]

Prior to the arrival of Europeans, Australian agriculture had developed its own distinctive practices, all geared to work with the naturally occurring landscape and to provide further help with water conservation. When the Europeans came, they mostly did not take the time to understand the farming methods of the Indigenous peoples. They simply seized the land and put it to work for themselves in the same way they would have done in Europe. But this land was different, and the consequences for their failure to understand that point have been severe. But it doesn't have to be that way.

THE EARTH, OUR MOTHER?

Hannah Arendt suggested that the modern age began with the rejection of God as Father and climaxed with the space race, which she saw as a rejection of the earth as our mother.

To many contemporary Christians there is something uncomfortable about the imagery of the earth as our mother. Doesn't it suggest an equivalence between God and the earth, as if the division between Creator and creation has been collapsed and the earth has been elevated to a godlike status? For the Christian, such a view is clearly wrong. God alone is the origin of life and stands above and distinct from his created order. So there can be no suggestion of an equivalence between God and his creation.

But we don't have to take the phrases *Mother Earth* or *Mother Nature* in that way. While we must never confuse the distinction between God and his works, there is something maternal in the way we relate to the earth—to what Pope Francis calls "our common home."[2] To describe the earth as our mother can be a way of naming our indebtedness to the earth, a way of making the particular forms of nourishment that flow to us from the world more tangible and concrete.

And there's actually some precedent in church history for talking about the earth in precisely this way. Tucked away in the book of Job is an odd verse that's easy to miss if we aren't paying attention. It comes near the end of chapter 1, after Job has received word from one servant after another that all his possessions and even his own children have been taken from him. Job grieves his loss and concludes by saying, "Naked came I out of my mother's womb, and naked shall I return thither: the Lord gave, and the Lord hath taken away; blessed be the name of the Lord" (Job 1:21).

For much of my life, when I read that verse, I thought Job was simply recognizing that we do not bring any wealth or power with us into the world when we're born, nor can we take whatever wealth and power we gain during our lives with us when we die. But that's not *exactly* what Job says. Job says that he came from his mother naked—that's obvious enough, we think—"and naked shall I return." So who is the "mother" Job is thinking of when he says this? It can't be his biological mother because he won't return to her when he dies. The American theologian and pastor Jonathan Edwards has the answer. Edwards suggests that the earth is "the common mother of mankind." The "mother," Job is referring to, Edwards says, is "the bowels of his mother earth, out of which every man is made." God is our Father, Edwards says, and the earth our mother.[3]

So Scripture itself teaches us to regard the earth as our mother in the particular sense that we are dependent on her to nourish us, and that in our very physical makeup we are made from her "body." Edwards isn't the only notable thinker in church history to speak of the earth this way. More recently, John Paul II used similar language:

> Once all reference to God has been removed, it is not surprising that the meaning of everything else becomes profoundly distorted. Nature itself, from being "mater" (mother), is now reduced to being "matter," and is subjected to every kind of manipulation. This is the direction in which a certain technical and scientific way of thinking, prevalent in present-day culture, appears to be leading. . . . By living 'as if God did not exist,' man not only loses sight of the mystery of God, but also of the mystery of the world and the mystery of his own being.[4]

Not only does John Paul II agree with Edwards that it is legitimate for Christians to refer to the earth as mother, but he also vindicates Arendt's point, that our sense of the mystery of God and the mystery of his world rise and fall together. Thus a Christian alternative to the revolutionary society must begin with a reimagined Christian conception of the earth, our common home. In articulating and living into this different understanding of the world, one based on a kind of filial piety that we owe our mother, Christians can present a different vision of humanity's relationship to the planet.

There are three keys to recovering this alternative understanding of our relationship to the earth. First, we must learn to see the earth as a fellow living creature that makes real moral claims on us. Second, we must develop a willingness to allow the realities of creation to disrupt our ambition. Third, we need to develop an ethic of kindly use in our relationship to the earth that sees the health and flourishing of the land as a nonnegotiable consideration when we farm, build, and so on.

RECOVERING OUR RELATIONSHIP
WITH THE EARTH

In one of the more famous scenes in his Chronicles of Narnia, C. S. Lewis imagines the Pevensie children and the beavers walking to meet Aslan at the Stone Table as spring finally breaks through in Narnia. The children are delighted, to say nothing of the animals who have been without a spring for far longer. They delight in the sound of melted snow dripping to the ground off tree branches, in the sight of flowers coming to life, and in the birdsong echoing through the woods. This is one of the first signs in the story that things will come right in the end, that the White Witch and her eternal winter will not have the final word. Spring brings hope.

But there's something that can easily pass us by as we read. Notice how many plants and birds the children are able to identify. A large part of the delight Lewis conveys in that passage only works because the children can successfully identify blue bells, thrushes, and other plants and wildlife.[5]

Most Americans today, myself included, would not fare nearly so well. Our inability to name plants and animals, a kind of botanical and animal illiteracy, is a common problem today for people raised in cities, who are more observant of our screens than of the natural world around us.

It does not need to be this way, however. Several years ago I visited another Bruderhof community, this one in upstate New York. I had the chance to tour their school. It was early spring, and as part of their work, the students were tracking how many unique species of local birds they could spot around their community. By the time I arrived, the list, which was hung up in one of the hallways of the school, stretched down nearly to the floor, with over sixty species included on it. The community saw play as among the most important things children do, and they also believed that much of their play should be out of doors. And so, because these were the norms of the community and because many parents in the community had also grown up there, the school's students had a remarkably broad knowledge of their local plant and wildlife.

This kind of knowledge is the beginning of a healthier relationship to the natural world. Before we can be more at home in the world (and before we can begin to address the looming crises before us), we must first learn to look at and name the world. Indeed, giving names to creation is one of the first things human beings do in the Genesis creation account. The point is not to see the world passively, as we might see a TV, but to look at it actively, with intention and knowledge. This requires patience, as well as a commitment to slow our lives down enough to make such looking possible.

But the rewards for even this simple act are significant. The late Clyde Kilby, who was a professor of English at Wheaton College, kept a list of resolutions he observed for the sake of his mental health. The list included, "Once every day I shall simply stare at a tree, a flower, a cloud, or a person. I shall not then be concerned at all to ask what they are but simply be glad that they are."[6] It's this kind of delighted looking at the world that we must recover.

It may seem like a small thing, perhaps too small for the scale of the problem before us. And, indeed, if this is all that changes, then it would be too small. But learning to see in this way is merely the first step toward a healthier regard for and relationship with the land. Because at present it is not the primary way that most of us look at the land.

As John Paul II notes, most people today see the world as a kind of organically generated mass of resources that exist for our consumption. This is the line Pedro de León took when he saw Peru, and it's the line we have been learning to take ourselves ever since. The world is something like a warehouse of goods for humanity's use. This approach reduces the planet to a kind of thing, as Weil warned—something voiceless and, indeed, lifeless.

These assumptions often show up in the way climate activists call on us to make changes in our behavior to help mitigate the damage likely to be caused by a changing climate. We are told that if we do not change the ways we use the planet, our lives will be substantially more difficult in the future. This is true, of course, but it doesn't get to the roots of the problem, for it suggests that our ecological problems can mostly be solved through superior techniques—more energy-efficient vehicles, for instance, or a higher usage of green, renewable energy sources and less dependence on fossil fuels. These would be great gains, of course, but they would not strike at the primary problem before us.

The chief problem with our posture toward the earth today is not technical but imaginative. Pope Francis explains the problem well, citing the work of the Eastern Orthodox patriarch Bartholomew I, who "asks us to replace consumption with sacrifice, greed with generosity, wastefulness with a spirit of sharing, an asceticism which 'entails learning to give, and not simply to give up. It is a way of loving, of moving gradually away from what I want to what God's world needs.'"[7]

It's true that our relationship to the earth will be more sustainable if, for example, we drive electric vehicles instead of gas-powered vehicles. But if we maintain the extractive logic that defines our relationship to the earth and simply find less tangibly destructive methods of extraction, we still have not actually solved the problem at the heart of our relationship to the earth, which is that we do not actually *have* much of a relationship to the earth. The child has become a stranger to its mother. And this estrangement is of more than just ecological significance. Francis's predecessor, Pope Benedict XVI, explained how this alienation from our mother actually hinders us in our relationship to God: "When God, through creation, gave man the keys to the earth, he expected him to use this great gift properly, making it fruitful in a responsible and respectful way. The human being discovers the intrinsic value of nature if he learns to see it as . . . the expression of a project of love and truth."

Whether it's green or less green, an extractive approach to the earth is still based in the revolutionary story that centers the self and empties nature and neighbor of their being and significance. Even a more eco-friendly posture toward the earth can be radically selfish, incapable of cultivating in us the virtues and habits conducive to a life of love and belonging.

THE WILLINGNESS TO BE OBSTRUCTED

If we are to recover an authentic relationship to the planet, then we must let reality chasten and refine our own ambition and desire. Being obstructed in this way is good for us. It can teach us to love, for what is love but the willingness to set aside our private desires in light of the need or desire of the other? To love is to be willing to be obstructed by the beloved. What does this willingness to be obstructed mean for our approach to the natural world? Several possibilities spring to mind.

First, a willingness to be obstructed will affect our food choices. The easiest way of eating today in America and in much of the West is to simply purchase what is cheap and easily prepared. As a result, much knowledge has been lost, and land and animals have been harmed as we have chosen easier ways of eating.

To be willing to be obstructed here means a willingness to spend a little bit more money on our food, if we are fortunate enough to have the budget for it. Spending more on ethically sourced meat is particularly significant. This one step can help undercut the degrading system of "meat production" that is now so common in American agriculture *and* help support the kind of farmers and ranchers trying to model a more God-honoring relationship to their animals. We should also—again, if our circumstances allow—be willing to be obstructed in how we prepare our meals. It is good to take the time to learn a bit about food preparation and cooking.

In allowing our "freedom" to be interfered with in this way, we're prioritizing the health of the land and animals over our own convenience. We're saying that it's more important that animals be treated well than that we save a bit of money by buying cheap meat brought to our tables via acts of cruelty, which we tolerate mostly because they remain hidden from view in factory farms and meat processing plants.

Obviously, this will be easier for those with larger incomes. But, even so, many cities have programs that make good food available. Early in our marriage, my wife and I availed ourselves of such programs often. Likewise, churches can help make this sort of relationship to our food more plausible for more people. They can do what two of our Presbyterian Church in America churches do in Lincoln and host food distribution centers on a weekly basis. Through a ministry called FoodNet, local grocery stores donate food that is going to expire within a couple days, and the FoodNet distribution sites give it away freely to anyone who comes.

Churches may also be uniquely positioned to serve as a network for skill sharing—pairing people in their neighborhood or community who possess practical skills with those who desire to learn. This could easily include a cooking class for teaching people basic skills around the kitchen, how to work with ingredients, how to prep some basic meals, and so on.

The flip side of rejecting an extractive logic in our relationship to nature is adopting a generative logic—a way of relating to the world that seeks to produce more life rather than suck away the life that is left. A generative approach to food will include doing all we can to make healthy food and healthy food habits accessible to as many people as possible.

It's not hard to imagine other applications of this same principle in other arenas of life. To be willing to be obstructed will mean sometimes sacrificing economic opportunity for the sake of nature or neighbor. We can even stretch the principle a bit and apply it to a variety of daily life decisions we make—how we will get from place to place, where we will live, the number of cars we will own. If we're willing to set aside the idol of convenience and allow ourselves to be obstructed in small ways in order to lay hold of some greater good, we will quickly begin to see the possibilities for living a life more closely bound to the land, more attentive to its need and its life.

AN ETHIC OF KINDLY USE

In his younger days, my dad was a great bowhunter. A couple of his trophies, including an arrow he once split with another arrow, Robin Hood–style, are still displayed at my parents' home. He was seldom happier than when he was sitting in a tree on a cold, late-autumn morning, his bow at the ready, surveying the fields around him and watching the sun slowly peek over the horizon.

Dad was a kindly hunter. If it was early in the season and he saw an adult doe in the field, he wouldn't shoot it, even if it was a perfect shot. The doe might have babies to care for. Likewise, if he saw a button buck (a young male deer), he would usually let him go too—button bucks needed to get old enough to breed and help renew the deer population. And even if he had a potential trophy buck lined up, if the shot was not favorable, he wouldn't take it. He wanted the kill shot, taken from an angle perpendicular to the deer such that the arrow could pass through the deer's vital organs and drop it almost immediately and with minimal pain. He would pass on shots at a bad angle that could maim the deer without killing it or that might fatally injure the deer, but only after a long, painful process of bleeding out as it fled across the fields. Dad wasn't simply trying to kill a deer any way he could for the sport of it. Nor was he trying to take a deer for its meat at any cost. If the cost of his food was a slow and torturous death for the animal, then the cost was too high.

It's this sort of posture toward the land that we all ought to adopt. Doing so is a matter of both will and knowledge. Dad's ability to know when to shoot and when not to, which deer to take and which to let live, depended on his knowledge—on him having spent enough time looking at the natural world to make wise choices. If we are not first attentive to the land, it will be impossible for us to adopt an ethic of kindly use.

Likewise, inherent in the idea of kindly use is the idea that I am not the only party involved in my use of the land. In other words, the idea of kindly use presupposes a willingness to be obstructed by lives other than our own. There were seasons, especially early in his hunting days, when Dad did not get a deer. He could've gotten one, of course, if he had compromised on his standards, taken the risky shot, taken the button buck, taken the mother deer. But he wouldn't. The life of the place had, in the words of Wendell Berry, come before his and would continue after his. And so, the standard for my dad's relationship to the place was first and foremost what was best for the land rather than simply what he wanted to get out of the land.

Ultimately, this ethic is an acting out of Hartmut Rosa's idea of "resonance," since it's premised in observing the world and allowing the world to act on us even as we act on it. It was the Reformed political theorist Johannes Althusius who said the purpose of our politics is to structure our relationships toward symbiosis: that is, toward mutual flourishing. Althusius was specifically referring to our human relationships, of course, but the concept has an obvious application to questions of ecology. Unsurprisingly, this same approach to the land has broader social, policy, and economic application as well, for it rejects the idea that our relationship to nature flows only one way—natural resources being extracted from the world and consumed by humans.

In his book *The Nature of Nature*, conservationist Enric Sala cites one example of extractive thinking, though he could've cited many others:

> Think, for example, of a rich tropical forest in Borneo, a mature ecosystem supporting one of the highest diversity of species in the world. Humans clear-cut it and replace it with an oil palm plantation, a monoculture with near-zero diversity. Only a scorched forest would be less ecologically mature than a plantation. The palm oil will be consumed in food products in cities around the world, but humans will not return anything to that ecosystem in exchange. As long as humans maintain the plantation, that habitat will never see a return to its former ecological glory, and the asymmetrical boundary between the forest and the plantation will persist.[8]

What would it look like if our policy decisions and our corporations' business decisions began with the assumption that we owe something to the world—that we ought to allow the world to act on us as much as we act on it? I can think of both small and large ramifications. I hope our office parks would look different—with more trees and garden space, at minimum, in a bid to maintain *some* biodiversity amidst the concrete jungle. Perhaps also our cities would look more beautiful, both because they could preserve more green space if we did not need so much space to accommodate our cars, and because planting trees and flowers in our cities is a delightful way to make the city unique and beautiful.

Of course, most of us will not be able to do so much, since the spaces we are able to influence are far smaller and more limited. Even so, I'm reminded of one of my mom's favorite children's books, the 1982 picture book *Miss Rumphius* by Barbara Cooney. It tells the story of a woman whose grandfather, on hearing of her many ambitions in life, added one final thing to her list: you must do something to make the world more beautiful. And so, in her old age, after she had traveled the world, after she had bought a small home by the sea, Miss Rumphius began planting small purple flowers called lupines. In her old age, Miss Rumphius could look out her windows and see the hillsides covered with small purple flowers. She had done what she could to make the world more beautiful. May we all do likewise.[9]

BEATING THE BIG DRY

And what of the Danthonia Bruderhof and their dry creek beds? They are dry no longer. What happened? They looked. They paid attention. They learned that some of the worst land on their farms had been subject to overgrazing for long periods of time. This suggested to them that whatever they needed to change, it would involve how they handled their livestock. And so they began to study and to ask questions.

They came across the work of a Zimbabwean ecologist who had puzzled over a similar problem in Southern Africa. Why, he had wondered, was overgrazing wreaking such havoc on Zimbabwean farms when herd sizes were much smaller than they had been historically? If we have fewer animals, why do we have an *overgrazing* problem? Eventually he found his answer: the predators were gone.

Whether in Australia or Southern Africa or the Great Plains of North America, livestock traditionally grazed in small, densely packed groups. They did this for safety. If they were scattered across the land, they were easier prey for lions or wolves. If they were packed together tightly, they were better able to protect themselves.

This dense packing had an effect on the land: by rapidly grazing small plots of land and then enriching the soil with their manure, these livestock effectively cared for the land and even created topsoil to aid farmers in their work. But with the predators gone, the animals had scattered and now no longer grazed one area, so their manure was not concentrated enough in any one place at any one time to have the same effect.

Upon realizing this, the Bruderhof purchased movable fencing and began creating a schedule for how they would graze their livestock in small, densely packed groups so as to produce the same net effect for the land as if their cows were fearful of a lion attack. Soon the soil began to be restored.

Another realization they had was that planting trees in strategic places would help enrich the soil, store water, and prevent water runoff, all of which made for healthier land. In the little more than twenty years that the Bruderhof has been living on that land, they have planted over a hundred thousand trees. Meier explains, "Trees impede wind as it travels across the landscape; the faster wind moves, the more moisture we lose. Trees provide habitats and shade. Where there are trees, the earth will absorb up to sixty times more rainfall than pastureland. Their roots pull nutrients up from far below the surface—a mature tree deposits 7 percent of its full biomass into the soil every year, which benefits shallower plants. And they are simply beautiful."[10]

Over the years, these changes have brought about a remarkable change in the land. Pictures from the early 2000s, taken shortly after their arrival, show a brown, dried-out land that even at a quick glance looks inhospitable to life. Photos of the same plots of land today show lush green grass and full ponds dotting the landscape. Where once there was death, now there is life. And isn't that how it ought to be among Christians? Meier says it well: "What we're doing at Danthonia to care for the land is not such a big deal. . . . Our calling is to live a life of discipleship of Christ, and to follow his path as best we are able. Caring for this land is simply a reflection of our desire to be true to Christ who loves the flowers of the field, sparrows, children; who takes pity on the sick and needy; whose heart is with the destitute and downtrodden."[11]

Christian ecology is merely Christian neighborliness applied to the land and to animals. It is to take up the yoke of Christ as we encounter the created world all around us. If Jonathan Edwards and John Paul II are right, it is to practice the art of listening to and caring for our mother.

8

A VISION OF CHRISTIAN BELONGING

The Household and the Sexual Revolution

In the fall of 1541, the Bubonic plague came to the southern German city of Strasbourg.[1] Over the course of the outbreak, around one in every seven people in the city would die. Considering how Covid-19 and its (relative to the population) low death toll rocked life in the United States in 2020, we can appreciate how devastating this plague would have been. When such calamities strike today, they raise obvious questions about God's goodness, and the pastors in a city facing such adversity are expected to have answers, even as they bear their own burdens of grief. It was no different in Strasbourg.

The leading pastor in the city was a man we met back in chapter six: Martin Bucer. Over the course of the outbreak, nine members of Bucer's household would die—two servants, a foreign boarding student, three older children, and, at year's end, two infant daughters. But the sorest blow would destroy the household itself: on November 16, Bucer's wife and the heartbeat of their home, Elisabeth, would die. By the time of Elisabeth's death, the Bucer family had become famous throughout the region. Martin had long been known as an advocate of church renewal, a keen evangelist for the Protestant Reformation, and a gifted institutional organizer. But by his own admission, none of what he did would have been possible if not for the industrious Elisabeth, a runaway nun he had married in 1522.

To capture something of the joie de vivre of their home, we might consider a record of its life left behind in a letter to which both Martin and Elisabeth contributed. The letter was sent to their mutual friend Margaret Blaurer, who lived in the Swiss city of Bern. Martin had written to her to answer a prior letter of hers. Near the end, he apologized that Elisabeth had not written to her. She did not like writing, he said, and also she was quite busy. In addition to hosting two Italian refugees, they had recently been joined by four French refugees and two German seminarians studying with Martin. Martin and Elisabeth also had a number of children—we don't know their exact number, but it may have been as many as eight. This household, overflowing with life both because of their own union and because of their radical hospitality, left little time for letter writing. But before the letter was sent, Elisabeth saw it and contributed her own lines at the end: "I don't mind writing at all, but the small fry never stops. Good night! Pray to God for us. Now I have to go to the kitchen."[2]

To say their home was full would be an understatement. And yet this was normal life in their household. Strasbourg, a large, well-off city close to the French border that offered broad religious tolerance, was a natural destination for French and Italian religious refugees seeking shelter. The Bucers were happy to offer it to them. Moreover, given the need to train pastors to lead the German church, and given the lack of seminaries equipped for that work in the early days of the Reformation, it was not unusual for aspiring ministers to live, like apprentices, with the family of the local pastor. This arrangement was found throughout the emerging Protestant world. Martin and Katie Luther also hosted many seminarians in their home in Wittenberg.

Martin and Elisabeth's marriage was an unlikely relationship in many ways. We know very little about it, as Martin was private about his family life. However, we do know that both Martin and Elisabeth had taken religious orders under a kind of duress—Martin joined the Dominicans at age fifteen in order to pay for his continuing education. Elisabeth was forced into the religious life by her family, who didn't want to provide the dowry that would have been required for her to marry. However they met, the two married in the summer of 1522. In 1523 they would arrive in Strasbourg. Over the next eighteen years, they would make a home in the city that would become famous as one of the warmest, most hospitable households in the area.

THE ISOLATION OF THE FAMILY

It has been fashionable for many years in socially conservative circles to regard the family as, to use a common phrase, "a haven in a heartless world." The idea has evolved slightly over time. When the phrase was first used, it was intended to describe a divide between the heartless world of the marketplace outside of the home and the virtuous sanctuary of home and family life. In more recent years, the phrase has often been used to draw a distinction between the supposed godlessness of American public life and the sanctity of family life. In either case, the family is seen as a kind of bulwark, a community still governed by love and mercy when all around it the world is governed by the iron laws of markets or the progressive ideals of the left.

That this way of seeing the family has become so common in conservative circles should not surprise us. If the world itself is basically violent, and our ways of supporting our lives in the world rely on our own power to take what we want or need even at the cost of others, then humanity has two choices: either normalize this sort of violence universally or try to keep it contained in specific areas of life through the use of other communities that follow other laws.

Thus, as the historian Christopher Lasch tells the tale, the nuclear family emerged in the nineteenth century as a means of correcting for the excesses of the world outside the home and for instructing in manners and virtue.[3] It was an attempt to have the cake of industrialism and eat it too—reap the short-term riches that come from an industrialized world *and* preserve the forms of character, integrity, and virtue that were still widely seen as good and desirable, even if somewhat out of place in the world of business.

This understanding of the home predictably worked itself out in heavily gendered ways, according to Lasch. It was not simply that there was a divide between the marketplace and the home, in which the home was expected to do the work of teaching virtue. There was also an imagined divide between men and women, with men increasingly identified with the violence of the marketplace and women with the quiet domesticity of the home. Thus, marriage and family life came to be thought of as the means by which naturally violent and even bestial males could be taught something of virtue, something of domesticity, by the naturally more decent women in their lives. Because the world outside the home had been industrialized and reduced to a dog-eat-dog battle of wills, the home was necessary as a respite from that world. One nineteenth-century woman explained this idea by saying that, "the world corrupts; home should refine."[4] All of this would, in time, come to contribute to Betty Friedan's idea of "the feminine mystique" that we discussed earlier.

These ideas are understandable given the violence unleashed on the world by the revolutionary society. But they are ultimately mistaken. They operate on the flawed assumption that the world is naturally heartless, cruel, and violent, and the role of the family is to be a kind of defensive bunker, a closed society in which the vices of the world are kept out and other forms of life together can be imagined.

This conception both misunderstands the nature of society more broadly *and* places a weighty and, in many cases, unbearable burden on families, which are asked to do far more than can be reasonably expected of most households. It also reduces the moral expectations for men while burdening women with the work of somehow civilizing the men in their life. Finally, it suggests that the sort of restful, loving communal life that all people long for is only accessible to those who are married, which seemingly condemns the celibate to a life of loneliness. This idea becomes especially cruel when one considers the question of same-sex-attracted Christians who choose to remain celibate rather than act on their sexual desires. If the nuclear family is the only haven, then what of those who do not live with their nuclear family or no longer have such a family?

The realities of life after the sexual revolution have heightened all these problems. If the world outside the home is regarded as a mostly heartless wilderness—and to the poor, the weak, and the marginalized in America, it certainly is—but the family likewise has been weakened by the sexual revolution, what becomes of communal life in America?

HAVEN OR FOUNTAIN?

It can be hard to imagine another vision of what the family and household could be. If the home isn't a haven in a heartless world, what is? If the world is not in fact naturally heartless, what is the family's role in it?

Pope Benedict XVI's words in an address he once gave called "The Human Family, a Community of Peace" help us answer that question. The family, he says, is a school for peaceable living, a sort of training ground in the life of peace that equips its members to bring that peaceableness into the world:

> The family is the foundation of society . . . because it enables its members in decisive ways to experience peace. It follows that the human community cannot do without the service provided by the family. Where can young people gradually learn to savor the genuine "taste" of peace better than in the original "nest" which nature prepares for them? The language of the family is a language of peace; we must always draw from it, lest we lose the "vocabulary" of peace.[5]

Viewed this way, the universe is a set of concentric circles, all spinning around, all making the same music, but with distinct parts. The household is ordinarily where we are first taught to love the good, where we first learn how relationships of necessary care can and ought to function. It is where we begin to learn to place ourselves in the lively world we receive at birth, to embrace a life of mutual giving and receiving, to participate in the liturgy of love that stands behind all of reality. The family is a kind of reversal of the logic of the sexual revolution—my life for yours.

The sexual revolution sought to guarantee equality and justice by leveling the sexual playing field. The revolutionaries saw that powerful heterosexual men were given a range of choices about how to behave sexually that were denied to most people. They sought to correct this problem by normalizing the experience of powerful heterosexual men across society, such that everyone enjoyed the same range of possibility that men did. In other words, the sexual revolution normalized a conception of sex in which the sexual embrace is chiefly about each private person's experience and in which sexuality is a chief means by which each individual person articulates their identity in the world. The supporters of the sexual revolution saw that powerful heterosexual men had broad license to think about sex in self-centered, even narcissistic, ways, and they (rightly!) regarded this as an injustice. But their solution was to advance "justice" by affording everyone the same right to selfish sex.

The icon of the family, then, is a repudiation not merely of the egalitarian move at the heart of the sexual revolution but of the selfish sex that powerful men enjoyed in America in the years leading up to the sexual revolution. The family says to us that the purpose of sex is the giving of the self to one's beloved, that the natural expression of love is not chiefly for the sake of my own self-expression but for the lifting up of the other. This reality sits at the heart of the family, of course, in the sexual embrace itself, but the lesson it teaches us applies to all aspects of family life: in the family we are taught that the good life is one of self-emptying, of mimicking Christ in his generosity and love for the world.

Thus the family is central to the well-being of society, but not because of a competition between society and household. It is essential because the family is our first introduction to the world, where we first learn to speak the language of peace. In a healthy society, the language we learn to speak at home is the language we go on speaking in our adult life in our work, our church, and our neighborhood. This is why Bucer referred to the family as "the fountain and nursery of good citizenship."[6] The family is not a defensive bunker against the wasteland of the marketplace; it is a flower garden, a seedbed for raising the sort of people who are able to love their neighbors. Flower gardens, of course, are never intended exclusively for the keeper of the garden; they are intended for the delight of everyone who passes by. So it is with the family.

THE ORIGINS OF THE HOUSEHOLD

Making sense of the household in our context requires particular attention to the role of sex in bringing a household into being. The common way to think about sex in the modern West is to see it as being chiefly for pleasure and, particularly, the pleasure of expressing your authentic self in its fullest, most intense way. Sex is ultimately a means of self-expression, which is to say it is interpreted as being chiefly for the individual. But this is not the Christian understanding of sex.

Christianity says that what we desire in sex is not merely pleasure or a personal experience of satisfaction, but something deeper. We desire union with another person. In sex, more than anything else we can do with our bodies, we are able to cast aside the divisions that can so easily condemn us to loneliness and isolation. Theologian and ethicist Matthew Lee Anderson writes,

> Sex seems to be about other persons—and specifically about our desire for union with them. In desiring another person, we glimpse them in a special kind of light. We see them as encompassed by an atmosphere of glory and beauty, which awakens a sense of reverence and awe. That glimpse is, in a certain way, a discovery of them as they truly are: we discover in that moment the mystery of their otherness and their irreplaceability to us. We learn in that moment we cannot swap them out for another as though they were an iPhone. When we desire to unite with the person in this way, no one else will do.[7]

Anderson says that this orientation toward the other has another consequence as well: like all good things, we do not want our union to end. And so we come to the role of children within the life of the household. The best way to think about the role of children in a marriage is as icons of the couple's love. The children produced by the union between a man and woman become tangible, enfleshed statements of their desire and their union. This is why, according to Christianity, marriage must be between a man and a woman; the point of sex is a sacrificial union with another person, and this union is designed to be fruitful. A union that is by design permanently sterile is not able to accomplish this.

The fruit that this union produces, the tangible evidence of love, constitutes the household, as father, mother, children, and perhaps even extended family are bound together in a shared economy that has grown out of their love. Thus when we say that married love is generative, we mean more than the fact that it is biologically reproductive, though we cannot mean less than that.

Of course, we live in a world afflicted by sin, and so natural designs are often thwarted not by the willful sin of human people, but by the unchosen consequences of living in a fallen world. Many couples are infertile not by choice, but because of something outside their control that prevents them from being able to conceive. Such marriages are no less valid. (Matthew Arbo's 2018 book *Walking Through Infertility* is a helpful book for those people struggling with infertility—and really for all Christians to read, given that, statistically speaking, we all know couples in this situation.) Likewise, in cases where the birth parents are unable to raise their child, it may be necessary that another family would adopt that child into their home. Indeed, adopted children and adoptive families are given a gift that others are not, which is the chance to showcase the unique love of God for his people, for Scripture sometimes speaks of God "adopting" his children. We were once *not* God's children, but we *become* God's children through adoption.

So the point here is not at all to devalue the marriages of infertile couples, or to assign a kind of second-class status to adopted children. Instead, we can say here what Oliver O'Donovan has said in *Resurrection and Moral Order*: that some forms of human love look back to the good of the created order as given to us by God, while others look forward to the hope of redemption when God will wipe away every tear and all things will be renewed.

Married love is generative because it calls forth the smallest, most local forms of human community, the forms in which we can most naturally learn of the good life, of virtue, and of what it means to love one's neighbor and to love God. The intimacy that calls forth new life also shapes the daily life of the home—it creates a place of trust, safety, and homeliness. When the primordial act of household formation is obstructed, when the partners withhold something of themselves from the other, this introduces a hindrance to intimacy, a hindrance to the very practices that make the home beautiful and life giving.

In a modern individualist account of life together, human communal living is an extended negotiation over where I get to use my agency and where you get to use yours, as well as what both of us can do with our agency. It is all necessarily contractual, centered on the individual's desire.

But in an older account of human community that presupposes given forms of shared identity and mutual belonging, the task of growing in maturity and virtue means learning how to draw together the needs of the community and the wants of the human heart. In an ideal scenario, need and want come together—what I most *want* is actually conducive to the life of the community, so that I can have everything I want and, far from depriving people around me of anything, the fulfillment of all my desires elevates the life of the whole community because my desires and the community's needs are intertwined. What this means is that communal living is not primarily a problem of legal negotiation but of heart formation. The greatest need for any community is not chiefly a sound body of law to govern it, helpful though that is in a sinful world. The greatest need is members with hearts shaped by the call to love, whose desires agree with the needs of the place and the people.

But if the problem is one of heart formation, then this raises an obvious question: How are hearts—the seat of human desires—formed? How do we learn to desire what is good? It is not chiefly through power. Power is sometimes necessary to protect us from ourselves or from others. But power wielded apart from relationship and knowledge can only shape behavior; it cannot shape the heart. Only relationships of love can do that. The Catholic philosopher and historian Andrew Willard Jones explains, "The father leads his son into virtue by knowing his son intimately. He knows his weaknesses and his strengths, his inherent temptations and his natural goodness. The father uses this knowledge to deploy his superior power effectively in the perfecting of his son. This is nothing else than the 'care of souls.'"[8] If the good life is found in recognizing one's place in the world and discerning how one's agency and talents can be used to serve the life of the world, then these are lessons best taught within bonds of intimacy and trust. These are lessons best learned in the home within the family.

Suppose you have a child who struggles with anger. How will that child learn to understand their anger, control their body, and either practice righteous anger or repent of their intemperance? Many communities can and will respond to this in some way. A school can give the child detention when he hits a classmate on the playground. Later in life, the government can imprison the fully grown child when he assaults someone in the street. But by their very nature, these communities can do little more than that. Why?

First, they are often quite large. A school might have several hundred or even several thousand students under its care. This forces it to adopt a certain pragmatism in how it handles misbehavior, simply because it lacks the time and resources to plumb the root causes of a student's behavior.

Second, large and impersonal institutions lack the personal knowledge needed to understand a student's struggles on the heart level. Large institutions can observe behavior, but they cannot usually know the heart.

In contrast, a household is small. Even if you have a large immediate family and several other relatives living in the home as well, it is unlikely that the community will be more than ten or twelve people. This means, first, that there is more time for each person—if a child's tantrum requires an hour to address, an hour can be given. Second, because the community is smaller and has more time for its own life, each member is also known more deeply. The government sees an angry young man who assaulted someone. A household can see a scared little boy, perhaps one who is not neurotypical, so that he registers sensory input differently than other children. The household can love that little boy, creating spaces of play that feel safe to him while also working with him to help him know how to respond to an overload of sensory input. But doing all these things well requires intimate knowledge, time, and love. In short, it requires a family.

The household, then, is generative not merely because it produces new life but because it is the sort of community able to study, discern, and care for the human soul.

THE CENTRALITY OF THE NATURAL FAMILY

There is a second reason for viewing the household as the central community in a healthy society. Pope Benedict argued that the family is the first community any of us experience and so, just on pragmatic terms, there is reason to record it as primary. But that is not the only reason to do so. Consider the problem of how a community of any kind grows. Most human communities are created through some sort of formalized agreement between people. Whether it is a business, a school, a local church, or a political body, all of these communities exist because a group of unrelated people decided to create a new community to do some shared project together. The family is not like that. The natural family is the only community that can reproduce itself without any outside intervention or without taking in people from outside the community and integrating them into the community. The family arises naturally out of creation as men and women have children and then need a means of ensuring that the child is safe and provided for. As such, the family is primary in any sort of political system; it is the most basic political community imaginable.

From this insight follows an important point: no other human community could be said to come *before* the family because the family alone arises out of creation as men and women have children and then seek to raise them well. One application of this, especially relevant in our own day, is that the government did not *create* the family but merely recognized it. The family is more basic than the government. Indeed, the government has very little power at all over the family, save in cases where the life and safety of family members is imperiled by the abuse of other family members. The family comes first because it naturally occurs in the world. The government comes later because governments, though accountable to the natural law, are created when people choose to form them. They only tangibly exist in the world when people take steps to establish and preserve them.

This point is of enormous significance in our day due to the rise of same-sex marriage and, more recently, emerging questions over parental rights and transgender children. Once a nation redefines marriage to accommodate same-sex couples, that nation has repudiated the Christian vision of family. Those who countered opponents of gay marriage by suggesting that the advent of gay marriage would have no effect on heterosexual marriage were gravely mistaken. Even a faithful, committed sexual relationship between two people of the same sex will, by its very definition, be a sterile relationship. A same-sex family is incapable of reproducing itself naturally. So when such a relationship is placed on the same legal status by the government as a heterosexual marriage, the implication is that marriages are created by the state's legal recognition.

Do you see what has happened? The family, which grounds society because it is the first place where we learn peaceable living, and because it is the community in which human love actually becomes incarnate through the bearing of children, has been replaced as the seminal social community. Its replacement—the state—is by its very nature defined not by peaceableness and love but by the use of violence and coercion as part of its responsibility to protect its members from violence and injustice. Thus we have shifted from a picture of the world in which the most basic community we belong to is defined by peaceableness and exists outside the world of institutions, and have moved into a world defined by coercion, a world that quite literally cannot exist apart from the sanction of established institutions. To affirm the legitimacy of same-sex marriage is to accept the stultifying, mediated world that comes to us only in prepackaged boxes handed to us by large institutions.

To affirm the primacy of peace in Christian social doctrine, and the innate wonder at the world that is our birthright as human creatures, is to stand against contemporary ideas about sexuality and gender, including the acceptance of gay marriage as a social institution.

SEX AND THE GOOD LIFE

While it is true that the household offers a tangible expression of Christian belonging, more needs to be said. The reason I began this chapter by focusing on the Bucer household is because the community in that home was more than just Martin and Elisabeth and their children.

The Bucers were constantly opening their home to guests, mostly refugees and seminarians, and these guests were also part of the Bucer household. Their home was always bursting at the seams. We have already talked about the marriages at the heart of households. Now we must talk about the other members of the household and the way they too offer an alternative vision of human flourishing contrary to the libertinism of the sexual revolution.

Too often in recent years evangelicals have responded to the excesses of the sexual revolution by trying to adopt the basic posture of the revolutionaries but within a Christian frame. The response of many evangelicals has been to look at the sexual revolution and say, "If you *really* want hot sex, try abstinence before marriage and monogamy after." Evangelical leaders ranging from Tim and Beverly

LaHaye to Ed Young to Mark Driscoll have sought to win the sexual arms race by showing that Christians have better sex. This has been a losing fight, as anyone who looks at polling data on attitudes about sexual ethics well knows.

We would do better to learn from the example of the early church. Like today's church, the early church found itself in a culture that was obsessed with sex and fairly hostile to Christian ideas about sexuality. But unlike today's evangelicals, who have often coped with this situation by adopting many of the values and habits of the surrounding culture, the early church leaned into the weirdness of Christian sexual teachings. In particular, the early church foregrounded the beauty and centrality of celibacy as an essential Christian witness in the life of the church because, while marriage spoke to the natural needs of people, celibacy spoke to the spiritual, the eternal. Marriage draws our attention to the good of the created order as it exists and is affirmed by Christ in his resurrection. But celibacy draws our attention to the good of the world to come, when we will no longer marry or be given in marriage, for we will see God.

If you survey the church fathers, you'll find many treatises on the holiness and beauty of virginity and chastity.[9] For the early church, marriage was a great good. It provided the space in which God's intentions for sexuality could be realized and enjoyed as well as the means by which the human family is reproduced and brought up to know the peace and joy God offers to his people. And yet marriage was not the only possible good a person could pursue related to sexuality. By embracing chastity, Christians could show the world that there is a greater love than that of a husband and wife or a man and his mistress. Chastity testifies to the love of God and the uniquely satisfying pleasure of giving oneself wholly to God's service, which one could do if freed from the obligations of marriage and family life. St. Ambrose, a spiritual father and mentor to St. Augustine, writes beautifully of this unique calling in his treatise on virginity, in which he comments on Matthew 22:30, where Christ says that in the resurrection we will not marry but will be like the angels:

> Virginity has brought from heaven that which it may imitate
> on earth. . . . And indeed what I have said is not my own,
> since they who marry not nor are given in marriage are as the
> angels in heaven. Let us not, then, be surprised if they are
> compared to the angels who are joined to the Lord of angels.
> Who, then, can deny that this mode of life has its source in
> heaven, which we don't easily find on earth, except since God
> came down into the members of an earthly body?[10]

The egalitarian nature of Christian marriage was something of an
atom bomb in Roman society, but it may have actually been the
Christian teaching on celibacy that was the more striking for many.

First, Christian celibacy suggests that, contrary to both the
Roman world and our contemporary world, sexual desires are not
actually boundless, nor are they uncontrollable. They can be laid
aside when one finds a love so great and all-consuming that sexual
desires are inferior to the delight of this new love—the love of God.
Contrary to those who would see "authentic" sexual expression
as essential to the good life, Christian chastity suggests that the
good life can be lived without any sexual experience whatever. In
our own day, when a "right to sex" is sometimes debated and a
crisis of intimacy and belonging is so obviously upon us, the
notion of a love greater than sexual love is itself a powerful witness
to the Christian faith.

But we can say more. Note what Ambrose says about this chaste
love. Where is its origin? And how do we know its true shape? Its
origin, he tells us, is in heaven among the angels. And we on earth
can know its shape and nature because this chaste love descended
to us in the form of Christ. For Ambrose, the celibate Christian is
partaking of the life of heaven in a way that the married Christian
is not and cannot.

But, Ambrose says, this doesn't mean celibacy is superior to marriage. Both marriage and celibacy are true goods, and there is no
sin in desiring marriage. But what Ambrose is saying is that the
celibate life is not a lesser calling for people unable to get married.

It is a vocation that mirrors the life of heaven itself; it is a means by which the life of the world to come—when all will be united in the joyful, exuberant love of God—is drawn down into the world of today. The celibate person, Ambrose says, is a kind of time warp that allows us to see into the future, when we will see God as he is and find all our satisfaction and delight in him.

In fact, Ambrose tells us, there is even a sense in which the church herself is a vision of chaste fruitfulness, as the church now lives in a sort of "celibacy," inasmuch as she has not yet been united to Christ at the wedding feast of the lamb, which comes at the end of all things in the Christian story. Today the church is a sort of holy celibate, testifying through her life that God himself is all satisfying. I suspect that if more churches held out such a vision of celibacy, they would be far more welcoming to single heterosexual people as well as same-sex-attracted people wrestling with the claims of Christian moral teaching.

Thus in talking about how Christianity refutes the sexual revolution, we are not simply talking about the husband and wife in a Christian household and how their sexual relationship confounds the revolutionaries by placing sex in its rightful place (though it does do that). We also must talk about the other members of Christian households and churches—the celibate people who, at minimum, are not yet married and may never marry. If Christians are to offer a credible alternative to the sexual revolution, it will be by presenting a comprehensive vision of Christian belonging that not only discerns the rightful place of the sexual embrace in the lives of human persons but also discerns the heavenly origins of the celibate life for those who are chaste. A Christian rejoinder to the sexual revolution will highlight not only how the revolution degrades the natural but also how it obscures the supernatural.

9

THE WORLD IN
CRACKED ICONS

Wonder, Death, and the End of All Things

On the evening of December 6, 2015, I went to my parents' house to bring them an anniversary gift I'd baked that night—a Swiss roll filled with a peach and apricot mixture and iced with apricot icing. My wife, Joie, and the kids had been out of town for the weekend, and I'd used the time for baking. It was their thirty-first anniversary: it had been thirty-one years since the day they got married in the house that had been their home ever since.

Dad wasn't feeling well. He'd been struggling with shortness of breath all weekend and had experienced several spells of chest pain. This had been a persistent problem throughout the summer, which had prompted him, after much cajoling from my mom, to visit the doctor earlier in the fall. They had diagnosed him with some blood clots in his legs, caused by a small hole in his heart, and scheduled him for what was, relatively speaking, a minor surgery on December 14. We were still nervous—heart surgery is frightening, after all—but generally in good spirits and looking forward to a Christmas that would feel closer to normal. It would be an especially meaningful one for us, because it was our new son's first Christmas, our son who was named after my dad. This would be Dad's first Christmas with a grandson and first Christmas with his namesake.

So we didn't worry too much about his health that night. We ate some of the cake and a cookie or two that his sister had brought by earlier in the evening. We watched a couple of funny animal videos on YouTube. They asked about how Joie's trip to visit her sister's family had gone and whether she was still planning to drive back the next day. Dad and I talked about some projects we wanted to attempt on the house that Joie and I had just bought, and which we hoped to close on in a couple months, pending the inspection. Then I gave them both a hug, said goodbye, and drove home.

The next morning I went to work. Around noon, our realtor called: the house had failed the inspection. The sale was off. An hour later my mom called. Dad had gotten worse, so much so that he wasn't able to walk up the stairs without stopping on the landing halfway up to catch his breath. She'd finally convinced him to go to the hospital. So they got in their van and she drove him to the same hospital where our son had been born eight months before. She said he was okay now and that I didn't need to worry, but she asked me to pray.

I went to see him after work and found him hooked up to oxygen and looking slightly pale but otherwise all right. He was in good spirits. They were assessing his condition and figuring out what additional treatment he needed beyond the drugs they'd already administered. It was only later that Mom and I learned that he had been in the process of going into shock. The blood clots, it turned out, were not limited to his legs. There were a large number of clots in his lungs that doctors had not caught during earlier testing.

But we didn't know that yet. So I left, got dinner, and then drove back to the hospital. His color was better. A few friends had been by to visit. A couple of his hunting buddies had brought a singing Elvis doll for his room.

Later, Mom told me that shortly before I arrived the doctors had given him a highly aggressive clot-busting drug that was meant to break up the clots in his lungs. The clots had been so severe that this extreme method seemed the only one likely to eliminate the clots, which, left to themselves, could have killed him. I kissed him goodbye and went home. Shortly after, Joie and the kids got back. We tucked our kids into bed, talked a bit about the trip, and then went to sleep ourselves.

A few hours later, around 2:30 in the morning, while I slept, Dad paged a nurse on the floor. He said he felt his side going numb. The hospital called my mom, who rushed there and spent about thirty minutes with him before he lost consciousness. Due to the drugs they had given him to deal with the clots in his lungs, Dad had suffered a massive brain bleed. There was so much blood on his brain that his brain actually shifted eight centimeters inside his skull. Having some knowledge of what was happening to him, one of the nurses warned my mom of what the future might hold. "It's going to be a long haul," she said.

I woke up at seven the next morning and found a voicemail from my mom—I had somehow slept through multiple calls from her during the night. Her voice was faint, and it was clear she was crying. She said there had been complications during the night. Dad was not conscious. They were taking him to a different hospital that morning, one just down the road from where Joie and I lived, for emergency brain surgery. I quickly explained the situation to my wife, texted my boss to say I wouldn't be in that day, and then drove to the hospital. Mom arrived a few minutes later—she had been following the ambulance from the other hospital. They rolled Dad in and took him directly to surgery before I could even see him.

We sat in the downstairs waiting area for about ninety minutes, waiting for word from the surgeons and wondering if the word would be "we lost him." I sent out a few text messages and emails asking friends to pray. A pastor and an elder from our church came by to see us and pray with us, as did a woman from my parents' old church. Sometime around 9:30 a.m., the surgeon came out. He said the surgery was successful and that Dad was now up in the ICU recovering. He said they had left a tube in that could drain excess blood on his brain so that the pressure did not build up again. Then Mom and I went up to the second floor, where we spoke with a doctor and nurse from the ICU.

They explained that he was not conscious, that he was recovering, and that they were in the process of cooling his body to 91.4 degrees Fahrenheit to help reduce the overall strain on his body and increase the odds of a positive recovery.

A nurse told us that it was impossible to predict what his long-term prognosis would be. She said two patients with identical health factors and an identical brain injury can respond in utterly different ways—one might make a full recovery and go back to work while the other spends the rest of their life in a hospital bed.

And so Mom and I went to the ICU and found Dad in room 217, intubated and with other various tubes and wires attached to his body, including a couple probes and a tube sticking out of his head. Half of his head had been shaved, and he now had an ugly cut where the surgeons had made the incision that had saved his life. There was an array of machines on one side of the bed, a couple of chairs on the other.

In the coming days, we would learn the meaning of nearly every number on every machine. We learned, as does most anyone with a loved one in long-term care in the ICU, to glance at the numbers every so often, trying to discern how he was doing in the absence of any other way of knowing. And so began three weeks, and then six months, and then twelve months that our family will never forget.

■ ■ ■

They kept Dad's temperature at 91.4 for five days—two more than they had originally planned because his initial response was so poor. Once his temperature had been successfully lowered, they began twice daily "sedation vacations," times when they dramatically reduce the sedation meds the patient is receiving and check for signs of brain activity.

They did this through a variety of methods, loudly calling his name or tightly squeezing fingers and toes to check for a reflexive response to pain. At first, Dad didn't respond at all. By the fifth day, he was starting to react, but his response was limited. In a best-case scenario, doctors said, we would try to wake him and he'd open his eyes. But that's not what we saw. He only responded if they squeezed his fingers and toes so hard that he developed bruises on his fingers and toes. Then his body would seize up—particularly, his shoulders would lift up toward his ears—in an attempt to withdraw from the pain.

These results suggested he had minimal brain activity—levels that usually meant he was not going to survive. The doctors kept him cold for those two additional days, the longest they could without risking other damage to his body, hoping that perhaps this added time might help improve whatever slim odds he had. In the midst of all this, I remember calling the state's Medicaid office to get information about what kind of coverage options we might have for long-term care. When I described his condition, the Medicaid worker said our best-case scenario was likely him living out his days in a nursing home.

During that first week in the ICU, Mom would arrive at the hospital between seven and eight in the morning. I would get there around nine. We'd stay there all day and then come back the next morning to do it all over again. We were inundated with visitors for basically the whole day—people paying tribute, expressing concern, wanting one more chance to see him. And so much of our time consisted of welcoming people and, for me especially, walking people back to visit, often with the assumption that this would be their chance to say goodbye. One man from church broke down by his bed when he saw him. It was and is the only time I've ever seen him cry.

Within a day or two it became obvious that the role Mom and I would both play during the day was to be a facilitator for other people, giving them someone to express their grief to, someone to be the recipient of the care they desperately wished to give but felt powerless to offer, given their own lack of control in the situation and my dad's comatose state. The evenings were when we could have our own time with him. Throughout this time, I can only recall two extended moments that I had alone with Dad in his room. One of my two nights with him, I sat by his bed and read to him—first from a few passages I especially loved in Tolkien's *Lord of the Rings*. It felt fitting, as there is much about my dad that reminds me of Samwise Gamgee—the easily forgotten character whose quiet virtue often goes unnoticed but who is actually the best person in the story. In the end, what rescues the quest is not the strength or greatness of the other heroes but the tenacious and unflinching goodness of Sam, who slays the great spider for love of his master, who storms the dark tower to rescue his friend, who carries his nearly dead master on his back when Frodo has nothing more to offer. Then I read from *A Divine Cordial*, a treatise on Romans 8:28 ("all things work together for good") written by the seventeenth-century Puritan Thomas Watson. The words were as much for me as for him: "As ploughing prepares the earth for a crop, so afflictions prepare and make us meet for glory. The painter lays his gold upon dark colors, so God first lays the dark colors of affliction, and then He lays the golden color of glory. The vessel is first seasoned before wine is poured into it: the vessels of mercy are first seasoned with affliction, and then the wine of glory is poured in."[1]

As I sat with my dad, I thanked him. I didn't know if I'd ever talk to him again, and so I made sure to tell him everything I needed to, even if he wasn't able to hear it then. I told him that he had kept faith with me, with my mom, with his people, with his place, and ultimately with God. I thanked him for the legacy he had left me, for being the sort of dad who drives out into all that dark and all that cold to rescue his child. I told him that I hoped I would leave something like it for my children, including our eight-month-old son who bore his name.

On our other night together, we did something far more mundane: we watched the Nebraska bowl game against UCLA (a game that remains the last bowl win for Nebraska, as I write this several years later). I remember thinking it was the kind of game he would have loved—UCLA was faster than us, certainly flashier. But we wore them down with a power running game. We were patient. We stuck to what we did well. We didn't make mistakes. And in the end, we won. It was a quintessential Nebraska victory, embodying all the best virtues of my home state, virtues that were deeply impressed on the life of my parents. Through all of this, I expected that this was a long goodbye, that God was giving us and our friends plenty of time to be with him before he was taken from us, a chance to say all the things that needed saying before the end.

Then something unexpected happened.

On December 23, only days after a doctor had advised Mom to begin making funeral arrangements, Dad woke up. He could only open one eye.

■ ■ ■

Six days after Dad opened one eye, he was transferred to Madonna Rehabilitation Hospital, a couple miles down the road from the hospital where he had spent the past three weeks. (He would eventually refer to those weeks as "the most expensive nap I ever had.") When he arrived at Madonna, he couldn't breathe independently, he couldn't swallow, he couldn't move any of his limbs, and we had no idea if he would ever make it home.

In time, other parts of his body began to wake up. With the help of therapists, he was weaned off the ventilator and began to breathe on his own. At first he was limited to a liquid diet, then a liquid diet with a thickening agent added to make it a little closer to real food. Eventually we were able to start bringing in some of his favorite meals. I remember once bringing barbecue in after I got off work.

Other parts of his body started to regain limited function as well. One day he reached across his body with his right arm and scratched his cheek. Mom was delighted and said, "Rob, you moved your arm!" prompting Dad to reply, characteristically, "I had an itch." One day a pastor and elder from their church came to visit, and Mom wanted Dad to show them what he had started being able to do again: pushing with his right leg. With their visitors seated, she slid over next to Dad's bed and propped up his right leg, pushing her palm against the bottom of his foot. "Push, Rob," she said. Nothing happened. "Push," she said again. "I'm trying," Dad said.

After a few more seconds of feeling no pressure against her palm, Mom dropped her head while keeping her palm against Dad's foot so that it didn't drop to the ground. She was remembering again the long haul that laid before them. She almost started to cry, wondering why the leg that had started to work again the day before now seemed unresponsive.

. And then she heard laughter. She looked up. Dad, even then someone who loved a joke, pushed her hand back with his leg and then started laughing again. Both visitors also started laughing, and soon even Mom joined them.

■ ■ ■

As part of Dad's treatment, my parents were invited to be part of a support group for stroke survivors and their caregivers. Often at these meetings, the survivors and the caregivers would break out into separate groups, as the experiences are quite different. For stroke survivors, the struggles are more obvious: how to regain what can be regained, how to keep working in therapy, how to live with the reality of what has been lost.

Caregivers, in contrast, struggle more often with fatigue and a different kind of despair. For spouses in particular, the work of being a caregiver to a disabled husband or wife can be incredibly taxing emotionally—and confusing as well. After all, your life has also been upended by their injury. They have lost their independence, but so have you—and you don't have a team of therapists trying to help you get it back. Your body hasn't changed. In theory, there is nothing stopping you from walking out of the hospital door and trying to reclaim a normal life—nothing besides your marriage vows, anyway.

Tragically, there are people who do precisely that. And while we might have some sympathy for people driven to such despair that leaving their partner feels like the only choice they have, we should also recognize that there's something grievous happening every time a partner walks away. This was the struggle one caregiver was dealing with during one of my parents' support groups. Finally, in a moment of honesty and deep despair, he said, "I didn't sign up for this!"

The trouble with saying that, Mom said later when she recounted the story to me, is that actually he had. To take marriage vows is to sign up for this. In binding himself to his wife, this man had signed up to be a caregiver whether he realized it or not. My mom knew this, and she stood by the vows she had made. She kept—and is still keeping—faith.

■ ■ ■

Five months after he first arrived at the hospital, Dad took his first steps since those he had taken into the hospital under his own power on that awful December day. In the video my mom took that day, he rose slowly out of his wheelchair with the help of two therapists, one on either side. He was wearing gray sweats—the easiest thing to change in and out of for someone with his lack of mobility—and a brown shoulder brace on his left arm to keep his shoulder in joint. Because his left side was still almost completely paralyzed, his arm hung limp, and over time that causes the shoulder to separate. He also wore a blue gait belt across his chest—a sturdy belt worn under the arms to help with getting up out of bed or a wheelchair. He also had on special shoes and ankle braces, which helped stabilize his feet and legs. He didn't (and still doesn't) have enough strength in his ankles to stand or walk without those shoes. Finally, stretched over the toe of the left shoe was a blue surgical mask, which was meant to reduce friction as he attempted to walk, which he would only be able to do if he could manage to swing his left leg forward from the hip, since he had not regained any motion in the leg itself.

Initially, as he rose, he just stood and looked around, braced by his therapists. Then he took a step with his right foot. The therapist on his left side gave his left foot a nudge and it slid forward. Another right step. Another nudge and slide with the left. And so it began. After ten steps he looked around for a moment and said, "Sorry they're so small."

Months before, back when he was first waking up and struggling simply to eat solid foods, I had been putting my daughter to bed. She was only three years old at the time. After asking a few questions about "Pa" and what was going to happen with him, her face grew serious. She looked at me and said, "One step at a time."

"What?" I asked.

"One step at a time. That's what we tell Pa."

And so we told him. And so he did—and does.

■ ■ ■

In time, Dad would move back home to the house that their marriage has made and belonged to since they took their vows in 1984. Their days are difficult—and were even prior to Covid-19. Dad is limited. Much of his left side remains paralyzed, which means he has been cut off from much that he loved in this world, not least the sight of a farmer's field in the early morning hours as he sat perched in a tree stand, watching for deer but watching, even more, for the beauty of God's world that he has loved with an ardor that I know God smiles on. Some elements of his calling remain the same: he is still called to be a husband, father, and grandfather. He can and still does help raise our children. He teaches our kids archery and talks to them about conservation and the natural world. He's the guy I call when I have car trouble or a home repair project that's stumping me. But much has also changed. In many ways, his chief vocation now is to bear witness to the sufficiency of Christ in his limited state. His life has, even more than what is ordinarily the case for any Christian, become a witness to the sustaining power of divine grace.

My mom, who has health struggles of her own, manages the household now—not simply the housekeeping, which she has always done, but now the finances and maintenance of the home while also being a full-time caregiver. I help as I can, as do a number of friends who have kept faith with them for many years. But there is no fairy-tale ending to this story, at least not yet. Dad will not, barring something entirely unforeseen, climb into a tree again in this life. Mom and Dad will not know the delights of road trips together. Mom will continue to carry the weight that only full-time caregivers can know.

So how do they continue?

■ ■ ■

One morning before Dad woke up in the ICU, back when we thought we might soon be planning his funeral, my mom picked me up on her way to the hospital. Though we had been together almost constantly since Dad's injury, we had not had many quiet moments to talk due to the constant stream of visitors. As we sat in the parking lot, Mom told me a story.

About a month before he went to the hospital and all this began, Dad had been feeling ill and was struggling to breathe. It was a Saturday, and he was planning to help a young woman they knew from church move some furniture. My parents had become close with her and knew a bit of her story—in particular that her father had not really been around when she was young. She had gone through practically all of her life without an older, nurturing male presence. Though I am my parents' only child, they still have a vocation to parent, and they often became close to people like this young woman who have never known the security that comes from receiving attentive care from their elders. So my mom had talked with her about many things, offering advice and counsel and direction, as she has done for countless others.

Dad, for his part, did what he always did: he made himself available to someone who needed help. He had made plans with this young woman to pick her up in his truck—an old white pickup that roared across town wherever it went and that he had painted himself with a winter camouflage pattern of light and dark browns. They would drive together to get the furniture, load it up in the truck, and bring it back to her house. But now on the morning of the move, he couldn't breathe.

Mom told him to stay home. "She'll understand why you can't come if you just tell her how sick you are," she told him as he struggled to the door, tied his shoes, and grabbed his keys.

As he left, he looked at her and said, "She's been disappointed enough by the men in her life. I'm not going to do that to her. I told her I'd help. I'm helping." And he went out the door. A few hours later, he came home. The furniture had been moved.

My mom looked at me in the car, tears in her eyes, and said, "That's the kind of man your father is." As is often the case in such marriages, it is also the sort of woman my mother is.

■ ■ ■

Why am I telling you all this? It's not because I see a closer focus on the family as in itself a solution to our culture's homelessness and search for belonging. This was the strategy of a previous generation of Christian Americans: to try to make the nuclear family itself a haven in a heartless world.

But that strategy didn't work for two reasons. First, the nuclear family isn't intended to be such a thing. The family is not meant to exist as a refuge of peace and shelter amidst a world that is violent and treacherous. Rather, it is meant to be the means by which the peaceful world is renewed and preserved. The family's face is not and cannot be set against the world. Instead, it's meant to look toward the same object as the world itself—toward the goodness of God's green earth, toward the peace God has made that governs the world, and ultimately toward God himself, the all-sufficient one, the giver of life. Ultimately, the family and the earth look together toward the consummation of the age, when the king will return and all these things will be set to rights. To presuppose a conflict or even an incompatibility between the life of the family and the life of the world is to condemn the family to failure because the family's life is inextricably wrapped up in the life of the world.

My goal in telling this story is more modest. In one of his essays, G. K. Chesterton promises his reader to set fire to modern civilization using only the hair of a redheaded orphan girl in the street. He begins by simply laying out a series of syllogisms, beginning with an argument about the necessity of a clean home for young children and ending with the redistribution of property. Then he says:

> That little urchin with the gold-red hair, whom I have just watched toddling past my house, she shall not be lopped and lamed and altered; her hair shall not be cut short like a convict's; no, all the kingdoms of the earth shall be hacked about and mutilated to suit her. She is the human and sacred image; all around her the social fabric shall sway and split and fall; the pillars of society shall be shaken, and the roofs of ages come rushing down, and not one hair of her head shall be harmed.[2]

Chesterton begins with the inviolable dignity of a small child and, from that starting point, tears down practically the entire social system of the Britain of his day for the simple reason that the social system did not respect that orphaned child's dignity. That fact alone was sufficient condemnation of that day's regime.

The story of one family in one place living faithfully amid difficulty for a long time might work in a similar but opposite way. Much of the reason for our homelessness today is that we have imagined the wrong world. We have imagined a world red in tooth and claw, cold and heartless, where the only way to basic personal safety, let alone any loftier goals, is to look out chiefly for yourself and to trust our society's institutions to watch out for you.

So we define our identities apart from any deep engagement with land or neighbor. This comes naturally to us, after all. We've been doing it for a long time. And when nature bites back, as it will, we bulldoze it. There are always more mountaintops to blow up to access coal, more streams to pollute, more habitats to destroy, more animals to kill in our quest for personal peace and affluence. And when exploiting the land won't work, we turn to other ways of building up ourselves without a regard for neighbor. We practice selfish sex and bounce through partners without vows, without fidelity, without fruitfulness. We even tear at our own bodies through drugs and surgery, all in search of a peace that we are made to know yet struggle to lay our hands on.

And now, as we confront a world that is rapidly warming and, ironically, becoming hostile to life, and as we confront our loneliness and anxiety and despair and mental illness—what then? More technology? More institutions? More liberation?

I want to think there's an alternative to this. We've talked already about the thrill of encountering reality, of what it feels like to run through a field as the air rushes past. That is one way of encountering reality. And yet, of course, if that's all we talk about in defending the wonder of reality and the goodness of creatureliness and creaturely bonds and affection, then it can seem a cheap trick. Youthful pleasures are easy to defend. The virtues of fidelity, even during times of unspeakable pain, are far harder to observe and, for many, much harder to imitate.

What I hope my family's story suggests to you is that there's goodness in bodily living, even when the body is broken. There is something true about binding our life to the life of the world, even if that requires giving up our love affair with the fiction of endless cheap energy. There is beauty in marital fidelity, even when it comes at a cost. There is something invigorating and delightful in allowing ourselves to be defined by our neighborhood and our neighbor, even when that means we lose some of our own autonomy. And if I can see, in the abstract, that these things might be good and even holy, I desperately want to believe that there are tangible examples in the world I can point to that legitimize and validate these hopes. And then I remember that there are—because I know my parents.

The eighth-century theologian John of Damascus suggests that icons can be a kind of devotional tool. They are not to be worshiped in themselves. Instead, they serve as a tangible way of first attracting our gaze and then deflecting it toward something else, like light ricocheting off a mirror. One need not agree with everything John says about icons to recognize the usefulness of the image.

Ordinary Christian people like my parents are a sort of icon of both Christian community and Christ's own love. Our vision can be bounced off them and upward toward something larger. Indeed, the image of light bouncing off mirrors is perhaps instructive. The ancient Egyptians would sometimes use mirrors as a sort of lighting trick, setting up an array of mirrors in a room so that one mirror could receive the light from outside and bounce it off the other mirrors, providing light for the entire room.

Ordinary people living faithful lives together in a place, bearing up under what cannot be helped and laboring to resolve what can, offer us a vision of how a renewed Christian society could begin. These people aren't a final bulwark against decay or the saviors of a Christian nation. They are images of light that can, in time, give light to everyone. For these icons work in both directions: They direct our attention upward, toward the source of the light they reflect. But they also give light to others, and if there are enough of them, they can illuminate whole rooms, perhaps even whole worlds.

10

POLITICS BEYOND ACCOMPLISHMENT

Toward a Politics of Care

In 1963 a thirty-four-year-old hospital nurse and her thirty-five-year-old husband, a lawyer, welcomed their third child into the world. This particular child was born with an intestinal blockage—a life-threatening condition that would make feeding the child impossible and eventually cause the baby to starve to death. However, through a relatively low-risk surgical intervention, the blockage could be cleared and the child could live.

The child did not live.

Why not?

Because the mother asked the doctors not to do the procedure, and the father acquiesced, saying the mother knew more about these matters. Why would the mother make such a decision? The intestinal blockage was not the only thing "wrong" with the child. The child was, in the language of the day, a "mongoloid." This is what they used to call children with Down syndrome, a term that, as Justin Hawkins rightly observed in his essay "Dignity Beyond Accomplishment," combined anti-Asian racism with ableism, noting a similarity between the slanted eyes of people of Asian descent and the similarly slanted eyes common in people with

Down syndrome.[1] The mother asked the doctors not to intervene to save the child's life because "it would be unfair to the other children of the household to raise them with a mongoloid."[2] And so the child was, according to ethicist James Gustafson, placed in a side room, where this small baby would starve to death over the next eleven days.

As Hawkins noted in his essay, it is hard to know where to begin with our outrage at this story. Are we more livid at the parents, or at the fact that this happened only fifty-nine years ago, within the lifetime of many Americans today? And yet, as horrifying as this story is, if we stop here, we will have stopped too soon.

In the paper he wrote that told this horrible story, Dr. Gustafson raised a hypothetical question about the case: What would the doctors have done if the child had not had Down syndrome and the parents made the same choice about not intervening to clear the blockage? Would the doctors have gone to court to save *that* child? Would they have tried to override the parents' wishes and clear the blockage, thereby saving that hypothetical child's life? The doctors said that, for that child, they would have intervened. So why did they not attempt such an intervention to save this child with Down syndrome? The response is as searing an indictment of the American way of life as I've ever seen: "When a retarded [sic] child presents us with the same problem, a different value system comes in; and not only does the staff acquiesce in the parent's decision to let the child die, but it's probable that the courts would also. That is, there is a different standard. . . . There is this tendency to value life on the basis of intelligence. . . . [It's] a part of the American ethic."[3]

This is where all our revolutionary, modernistic thinking will eventually lead us. If there is no natural order in the world, if there is only raw matter and our quest to take control of it and bend it to our needs and desires, then those people who lack the ability to exert their will on the world in that way have lives that are simply not worth living. There is no room in such a world for the weak or the poor or anyone, really, who is unable to exercise the requisite force and agency required to take control of the world. A life's value is derived from the person's ability to project meaning onto the world, to define their own concept of life, meaning, and existence. If they cannot do that, what would their life even be?

This obviously is not in any way a Christian habit of mind. It is rather the opposite: the very thought of ascribing value to human life on this basis is demonic. And yet here we are. Indeed, here we *still* are. While we have adopted gentler language to describe people with Down syndrome in the decades since 1963, our treatment of them has, if anything, gotten worse, not better. As countless studies have made plain, we still live in a society that would sooner kill the unborn child that is likely to have Down syndrome than make a place for that child in our homes, in our cities, in our nation. One story in *The Atlantic* looked at the fate of babies with Down syndrome in the Western world and found that 88 percent of unborn babies who test positive for Down syndrome will be killed before they can take their first breath.[4]

But this problem is not unique to how we deal with those with Down syndrome. The broader issue is this: because a certain level of agency and accomplishment is treated as the sine qua non of the good life, people who lack a list of accomplishments that they could proudly print on a resume are, at best, relegated to a kind of second-class status. The disabled are killed before they can be born. The elderly are put out of sight and out of mind. The poor are relegated to specific neighborhoods where the wealthy and accomplished will not have to interact with them regularly, except perhaps when they drop off their groceries or give them a lift to the airport.

Caregivers, meanwhile, are likewise underappreciated and ignored because care-related work is, similarly, not valued. This is the founding assumption of the society we live in today in the Western world and particularly in the United States. The Christian church, if we are to have *anything* at all to say to such a world, must both unashamedly and comprehensively reject this value system, and we must model among ourselves an alternative value system that provides a healthier and more beautiful account of what we can expect in our life together with our neighbors. That is the task before us in this final chapter: How should we imagine a political society that would be ordered toward care rather than accomplishment? A second question follows from this one: How can we speak about the gospel and live as Christians in a society that thinks it is post-Christian but was never actually all that Christian to begin with?

CHRISTIAN SOCIETY IN THE WORLD

If you take the Metro-North line for ninety minutes out of Grand Central Station in New York City, you'll come to a small town called Beacon. When you get off the train, you'll see the Hudson River snaking along to your west. About twenty minutes west of Beacon, you'll find a place called Fox Hill. It is a community of Christians that belong to the Bruderhof, the same group that we met in chapter seven. Theirs is a society of Christian pacifism and, one might say if one wanted to be cheeky (and many in the Bruderhof do), Christian communism. When you join the community, you renounce both violence and private property and take lifetime vows to stay with the community, participate in its life, and promote that life to the best of your ability.

If you visit Fox Hill, you'll find a place that seems to be what anyone ought to mean when they use the word *idyllic*. There are gently sloping hills, lovingly maintained grounds, attractive meandering brick paths throughout the property, meadows filled with flowers (this is what my daughter noticed right away on her first visit), and people that greet you with a warmth that, at first, seems put on.

It is not.

As you spend more time there, the depth of the community announces itself over and over again. If you are fortunate, you will join them for one of their worship services, where you will hear hundreds of people of all ages spontaneously and from memory break out into joyful singing in four-part harmonies. Imagine a kind of Sacred Harp choir and you have the general idea.

Then you might tour the factory that provides them with their income and most of the members with their work. Perhaps you come across an oddly shaped work bench, noticeably lower than the others and perhaps featuring some other modifications, whose purpose is not immediately obvious to you. This, they will tell you, is where an elderly member of their community works, or perhaps it is a workstation for a disabled member.

The lesson is clear: because God's family has room for everyone, our family does too. "Making room" for people isn't simply a matter of saying the right things but of taking practical steps to *actually* include the weak, the disabled, the elderly, and so on. And so, as you tour the factory where the community makes the toys and furniture that provide them with an income, you find modified work benches and workspaces. The statement "everyone belongs here" is not just words for the Bruderhof. It is reflected in the physical spaces that the community lives in and shares with one another.

This is one way, though admittedly an unusual one, that Christians have tried to find their bearings in the world together and to offer an alternative to the heartless value system of contemporary America. It is how this community of believers has attempted to live lives of ordinary faithfulness and piety in community.

Some might fault the community for "withdrawing" from society and rendering themselves evangelistically impotent. But members of the community will insist that outreach can be most daring when the center of the community is most strong. It is precisely because they prioritize the needs of their community that they are able to welcome others into it and to serve their neighbors in a myriad of ways.

Others might say that this is a utopian project. If they've read certain books, the words "over-realized eschatology" might escape their lips, or perhaps something about "immanentizing the eschaton." To try and create a community of this sort before Christ returns is, according to these critics, neither wise nor possible. And yet there they are: nearly 250 people of all ages and many ethnicities living in community together in upstate New York, holding all things in common, healing the land, and recognizing that, as the title of one of the books they have published puts it, "everyone belongs to God."

Stanley Hauerwas has said that "in a hundred years, if Christians are identified as people who do not kill their children or the elderly, we will have done well."[5] The Bruderhof are a real-world expression of this basic commitment to life. Say what you will about their socialism or their pacifism. Accuse them of being utopians if you like. Fine. Yet never forget this simple fact: there has never been any thought with them that certain lives are not worth living. No one from the Bruderhof has ever been left to die because of a disability or shunted away to live out their final days out of sight and out of mind. They do not push their poor into designated parts of the community so that their wealthy needn't see them—indeed, they do not have poor or wealthy for the simple reason that they do not have private property. Unlike the "American ethic," which far too often has been uncritically accepted by American Christians, the "Bruderhof ethic" hasn't led to the screaming, agonizing death of eleven-day-old babies. And it is for all these reasons that I think we would do well to learn from their example. If we do, the American church could become the seedbed of a renewed community, bound by love and honor, and sufficient to meet the challenges of our time. But if we are to do such a lofty thing, we will need to adopt a way of living that may feel quite alien to many of us. Put another way, we American Christians from more assimilated Christian communities would do well to listen to the voices of churches and traditions that have *never* been part of the American mainstream. The way toward the faithful renewal of common life is to become "almost Bruderhof."

HOW TO BE ALMOST BRUDERHOF

As you have been reading, you may have asked yourself or desired to ask me this rather obvious question: Why not simply join the Bruderhof or some similar Anabaptist commune that lives according to such radical rules of life? Here is why: the only reason for a Christian *not* to belong to a community like this is because they think the Bruderhof expects not *too much* from our life together but *too little*.

Here the example of Martin Bucer, who we met in previous chapters, is helpful. Bucer had relationships with virtually all the major Anabaptist leaders in the Reformation, since they all passed through Strasbourg at one point or another because of the city's generous religious liberty policy. Indeed, at a time when many Reformers were persecuting the Anabaptists, Bucer loved many of them dearly and labored, as much as he could, to maintain positive relationships with them.

To take only one example, after the martyrdom of the Swiss Anabaptist Michael Sattler, Bucer publicly recognized him as a brother in Christ, calling him "a dear friend of God" and praising his sincere faith and piety. Such a comment would have been unthinkable from virtually any of the other major Christian leaders, Protestant or Catholic, in Europe at the time.

And yet, for all his love for many of their leaders, Bucer held this against the Anabaptists: He believed that their decision to separate from the established church of Strasbourg and begin their own independent congregations was a failure of Christian love. It disrupted the life of the city by breaking the fellowship of the church with the city. Moreover, it effectively quarantined many of the city's most devout believers from the rest of the life of the city.

For Bucer, Christian love isn't exclusively about actions one takes toward one's brother or sister. It is also about association. Bucer believed that by withdrawing themselves from the church and the civil life of the city, the Anabaptists failed to uphold the command to love their neighbor. Loving neighbor wasn't simply about willing their good or acting with love toward them in individual, one-off situations. It was about a persistent willingness to associate with one another, to uphold the life of the city and the good of all, particularly the poor, by maintaining the relationships that made the city strong.

What is needed today is for Christians to be committed to their cities, neighborhoods, and home places, as Bucer was, while tying those commitments together with the devout piety and generosity of the Bruderhof.

We might say it this way: if monasteries are places dedicated to work and prayer, the spirit of the Reformation says that all the world ought to become a monastery—communities of people defined by good work and prayer. The Reformation sought to throw open the windows of the church and take the gospel into all creation, elevating the ordinary Christian living of regular believers and calling all people everywhere to lives of Christian discipleship. It is because we have failed in this work that the ethic of worth via accomplishment has become ascendant in our culture. It is only if we, through the aid of the Holy Spirit, succeed in this work that this same "American ethic" will be cast down into the hell it deserves and from which it came.

How can such a work be done? There are three values of the Bruderhof that Christians of all sorts ought to learn from and adopt in their own communities. If we do that, then we can begin to plant the seeds that can, in time, grow into a renewed world marked by care, not accomplishment.

WHO BELONGS?

As he lay on his deathbed, Martin Luther spoke his final words: "We are beggars, this is true." And so it is for the Christian community: anyone who knows themselves to be a beggar, desperately in need of grace, belongs.

This understanding of communal belonging has two effects. First, it is a bracing rebuke of the spirit of our own day, which sees a kind of generalized acceptance of people's self-chosen identities as being not only a matter of personal kindness but of public justice. Indeed, there is something instructive in the role that the idea of "pride" plays in contemporary identity politics. In the Christian community, our eyes are constantly drawn toward our need, our inadequacy, and the all-satisfying, all-restoring grace of God. In Christian community, we are brought low so that we can be lifted up. In more contemporary communities, such as they are, our membership begins, as a popular sign I see a lot around Lincoln puts it, by claiming that "you are enough." It is perhaps not surprising that our communal lives are often so barren, for the posture of pride, the posture that says, "I am enough," is not a posture conducive to neighborly life.

The second effect of recognizing our own need is that it empties the members of the community of any sense of superiority. A close friend of mine used to pastor in a rural Presbyterian church. Like many old rural mainline churches, the church had its signature families—the wealthy landowners whose names might be on a wing of the building and who had been attending for as long as the church had existed. Early on in his time at this church, my friend faced a challenging pastoral situation with one of these families in his church. The problem, if one can call it that, began when one of the younger members of the family and his wife met with my friend to discuss baptizing their newborn child.

My friend was pleased to meet them and eager to hear about their relationship with Christ, what God was teaching them, their desire to raise their child as a Christian, and so on. So he began by asking them about their practice of their faith, involvement in the church, and so on. There was an awkward moment of silence. The husband and wife looked at each other and then back at my friend. The husband smiled and chuckled softly. "We don't need to talk about any of that," he explained. "I'm a _____," and he gave his last name.

Too often when wealthy families have said such things in church meetings, they have received the desired response: instant deference. Too often wealth and connection have been a ticket to privileged status in the church. But my friend wasn't fazed by it. "Well, no, we *do* have to talk about that," my friend said. It soon became apparent that neither the husband or his wife were in any way serious about their faith, that they did not have any intentions of attending church regularly, and that they had no sense of remorse or guilt about any of this. Getting their child baptized in this church was simply an item to check off a list in their family. But my friend wasn't having it.

Each of us comes to God with the same need and must receive the same cure. Recognizing this will have a radical flattening effect on our community *and* a radical unifying effect. Whatever our differences in ability, wealth, age, race, or anything else, each of us is a beggar, incapable of saving ourselves. The gospel that we hear and respond to in faith is a gospel that leaves no room for personal favoritism, racism, or classism, or for the notion that if I accomplish enough, then I can become a member of the community or perhaps a uniquely important person within it.

There is one final thing we should remember here: If all of us come to God with the same need, then every person we meet every day we are on this earth might one day rejoice with us in paradise. They might be or might become our dearly beloved brother or sister in the Lord. And so there can be no room for looking down our noses at those outside the church, no matter how ugly their sin, no matter how far they might seem from God. "Such were some of you," says St. Paul. And we must listen.

WHO GETS WHAT?

A friend of mine who has been involved in addressing a number of difficult cases of serious sin in local churches has observed that one of the worst things about sin is that it robs us of time. If you have ever been involved in working through the fallout of serious sin, you'll understand this. The time spent meeting with the person who is in sin, the time spent helping them seek reconciliation with the people they hurt, the time spent with the victims of the sin—all of this adds up.

That time could have been spent in other ways—enjoying a movie with your family; having coffee with a friend; spending an evening in quiet thought with a book, a good drink in hand, and a pleasant record playing in the background. The world is overflowing with pleasures for us to enjoy, if we have the time to enjoy them. But all the possibilities that flow from these good uses of time are lost when we must instead dedicate our time toward confronting serious sin and pursuing reconciliation or restoration between the parties involved.

But if sin has a way of stealing time and constraining us in our ability to love neighbors and do good work, then virtue works in the opposite direction. Virtue helps create time and opportunity to serve. If virtue, in a general sense, refers to traits and characteristics that agree with God's law, then it would encompass things like generosity as well as what the Puritan minister John Winthrop called "a native sensitivity of our infirmities and sorrows."[6] This availability of time, money, and even the members themselves is a signature mark of the Bruderhof.

To take only one example, there was an incident several years ago when an author with the Bruderhof's publishing house, Plough, was visiting the United States with his wife from their home in Western Europe. While over here, the husband became sick and there was some concern that he might need to go to a hospital to receive care. This created a number of problems, not only for the events scheduled but also for the couple—their home nation offered free government-subsidized healthcare to all its citizens, so the couple did not have any privately purchased health insurance normally and had not purchased any travel insurance prior to their trip. Given the nightmarish realities of the American medical system, this could have been disastrous for them due to the probable cost of care. But it wasn't. Why not? Because a doctor who belonged to the Bruderhof was able to go stay with them for several days to monitor his situation. Because of this, what could have been an enormously expensive medical emergency actually turned out to be a relatively minor incident, the only major financial costs coming when they had to bump their return flights back a few days due to his illness. Relative to what might have been, these costs were trivial.

This example is illustrative of a broader point: when our lives have a certain degree of elasticity to them, we are better able to love and serve one another because a large part of loving and serving is simply a function of availability. Too many people *desire* to be good neighbors, good sons or daughters, church members, and so on, but simply don't have the space in their schedule. In some cases, this lack of availability is the product of choices—choosing to take a promotion that came with higher pay but also far greater demands on your time, choosing to fill your children's schedules with after-school activities and sports, and so on. In other cases, such frantic living was not chosen but simply happened as the result of other circumstances—perhaps a disabled family member requires round-the-clock care, or simply making ends meet requires working several jobs. Whatever the reason, the outcome is that we are not as available to love and serve our neighbors as we would like to be.

What can be done to combat this problem? The psalmist tells us that "the earth is the LORD's and the fullness thereof" (Psalm 24:1). Construed this way, then, there is actually no such thing as private property, if by private we mean "property that I possess an absolute and inalienable right to use in whatever way I choose." The claims that God places on our lives condition the claims we can make as to how we use our property. This is somewhat akin to the relationship my children have to their allowance money. We give it to them, and it is "theirs" in the sense that they can choose how they wish to spend it. However, their right to dispose of their property is not absolute but is rather defined and shaped by the rules that my wife and I give them for how they use their money.

Obviously, one way of offering up one's property (and one's work) to God is to simply do what the Bruderhof have done: renounce private property and share everything in a common purse. But this is not the only way. Indeed, one of the ironies of much contemporary thought is that while Calvinism is frequently blamed for the development of modern workaholism and financial stinginess, the historic Calvinists themselves may be some of our best models for how to approach our property with a spirit of radical generosity while still maintaining some conception of private property.

Though it is most known today for its use of the phrase "a city on a hill"—which has since been invoked by many American presidents, including John F. Kennedy, Ronald Reagan, and Barack Obama—John Winthrop's 1630 sermon "A Model of Christian Charity" actually has a great deal to say about generosity and liberality with our money in particular.

If we . . . embrace this present world and prosecute our carnal intentions, seeking great things for ourselves and our posterity, the Lord will surely break out in wrath against us, and be revenged of such a people. . . . If our hearts shall turn away, so that we will not obey, but shall be seduced, and worship other Gods, our pleasure and profits, and serve them it is propounded unto us this day, we shall surely perish out of the good land whither we pass over this vast sea to possess it.[7]

Winthrop's words here, which among other things describe "profit" as a false god, are not unique among the Calvinist tradition of evangelical Protestantism. Calvin himself could be no less severe when dealing with those who cling to money and possessions. Calvin makes the point that generosity for the Christian is not something we show only to other Christians or only to those we owe something to. No, because everyone is made in the image of God and because all of us are need of the same grace, we are obliged to everyone:

Whoever, therefore, is presented to you that needs your kind offices, you have no reason to refuse him your assistance. Say he is a stranger; yet the Lord has impressed on him a character which ought to be familiar to you; for which reason he forbids you to despise your own flesh. Say that he is contemptible and worthless; but the Lord shows him to be one whom he has signed to grace with his own image. Say that you are obliged to him for no services; but God has made him, as it were, his substitute, to whom you acknowledge yourself to be under obligations for numerous and important benefits. Say that he is unworthy of your making the smallest exertion on his account; but the image of God, by which he is recommended to you, deserves your surrender of yourself and all that you possess.[8]

When this sort of generosity is normalized across large groups, as it has been within the Bruderhof, you find something interesting. If one of the chief obstacles to our ability to love and serve is a lack of time, money, or other resources rather than necessarily a lack of will, then as generous service to neighbor is normalized, scarcity becomes less of a problem. In many Christian communities the hindrances to care are not *actually* an overall lack of time or money but that the amounts of time, money, competence, and so on within the group are not broadly distributed. When generosity is normalized, the excess is shared across the group. And once that happens, many other good consequences begin to follow.

When we have what we need to feel cared for and to feel as if our daily life is mostly manageable, then we encounter our neighbor from a position of stability, even strength. And this not only takes away some of the fear we might have of a neighbor or some other unknown party; it actually equips us to serve them more generously because we ourselves are provided for. The Bruderhof doctor could travel to care for the writer and his wife because her own community was provided for and because she herself had the luxury of a job that did not require extensive time in the office, advanced notice of time away, and so on.

We might put the matter this way: Generosity begets generosity because, when we are generous, we are following our nature, which is to live in healthy relationships of mutuality in God's created world. Healthy mutuality begets healthy mutuality. And all this flows from the founding recognition of all Christian community, which is that we are needy, frail people whose greatest need is met through Christ and who are now called together into community with our fellow beggars.

What all of this means is that it should be normal in the Christian community for us to be giving to one another and serving one another in tangible ways with time and, yes, money. The Christian community should, as a normal part of its life together, assist the elderly with their daily care, support young families with childrearing (including babysitting), and rally around its younger members as they establish themselves and form households. When we do this well, we create a community of provided-for people who are in turn able to provide for others.

WHERE DO WE LIVE?

A large portion of what makes life together possible is simple geographic proximity. If it is easy to see your friends regularly, you are going to see them more regularly. And it is much easier if they live a few blocks away than it would be if they lived on the other side of town, let alone in another city or state. Indeed, a large part of successful communal life is a sort of incidental community, the sort that arises when, as I once heard someone say, "we have friends that we do boring things with." Anne Helen Petersen has written about what she calls "errand friends," which are, as the name suggests, the sort of friends you do banal, everyday things with, such as picking up dry cleaning, helping address wedding invitations, getting your car's oil changed, or making a quick run to the bank. "It's unremarkable," Petersen writes. "It's just life, but with another person there."[9]

Errand friends will most naturally be the friends that live close enough to allow for the spontaneity that errand friendships thrive on. You can't invite a friend to ride along with you while you go grocery shopping if simply getting to and from the friend's home will add forty-five minutes to your trip. If for no other reason than sheer pragmatism, a certain degree of proximity is essential for common life to occur on a day-to-day basis.

Yet we can press the point a bit more, in fact, because when we talk about geographical proximity, we are inherently talking about places and the difficult but worthwhile work of building places that are delightful and life giving. Here it may help us to return to the work of Jennings, who we have cited in previous chapters.

Central to Jennings's critique of whiteness, which is in many ways a critique of Western modernity, is the question of geography. What concerns Jennings when he considers questions of race and colonialism is that geography is basically irrelevant to the colonial mind—one place is as good as another, and no single place has any unique demand on individual people or for specific forms of care or attention. We have seen already the fallout of this indifference to place in history. Not only was nature denied its voice in helping to define and shape our modern sense of identity, but also the planet itself has withered under the oppressive forces of the late modern world, virtually all of which are utterly indifferent to landscapes and geography, the sorts of particularities that make a place what it is.

The result of this has been a pervasive loss of identity and agency across racial groups, though it has manifested in different ways, as people have been cut off from sources of identity outside of the sovereign, detached self: "The point here is that racial agency and especially whiteness rendered unintelligible and unpersuasive any narratives of the collective self that bound identity to geography, to earth, to water, trees, and animals. People would henceforth (and forever) carry their identities on their bodies, without remainder."[10]

In the era of colonial modernity, human identities are infinitely fungible and are expressed primarily on the body. This creates an enormous burden for people not only to articulate their own identity to themselves, which would be burden enough, but to then express that identity in an authentic way through their bodies. We should not be surprised that such a world is a breeding ground for mental illnesses and eating disorders while also being uniquely vulnerable to the abuses of the capitalist market—there is good money to be made in selling people the means they need to create their own identity, after all.

ROOTED AGAIN

The Christian community can offer an alternative to this trap. In moving closer to one another, we should not simply be seeking to make our own friendships closer and more convenient, though that is a fine goal. We should also see the decision to move closer together with other Christians as a way of loving the places that we share together, of serving the good of our non-Christian neighbors in that place, and even of making the place itself healthier. By attending to local places and sharing in the work of revitalizing them, we can learn to submit ourselves, including our desires and our ambition, to ways of living that are larger than any single person or family but constitutive of larger, broader communities.

What this will require is not simply that we seek to live in close geographic proximity to neighbor, though it will require that, but that our moving and our relationship to the places we move be grounded in something other than a simple desire to live near friends. Doing this well will mean not simply geographic proximity to our fellow Christians but a commitment to a shared project to see our neighborhood, town, or city thrive.

We cannot see our homes as standalone entities detached from anything else. Rather, we must see our houses and those of our fellow Christians who live nearby as instances of a common work to make the world more beautiful and to look more like God intends. It is, indeed, a literal remaking of "the commons," a term which we today think of as an abstraction but which, historically, was an actual space that was shared by the members of a village or town.

In premodern England, the commons was where small farmers could put their animals out to pasture, but it could also be the site of communal gatherings or brief neighborly encounters as one went about one's work. The loss of the commons has played no small part in the loss of the sort of boring, incidental friendships described earlier. For there are now few shared spaces in which we can encounter our neighbors—offices are not designed with the goal of creating authentic community, and third places (such as coffee shops, bars, and restaurants) are accessible only to those with the income to frequent them and who naturally enjoy such places.

The commons has been lost over the past several hundred years to enclosure as private people have closed off places, sealing them away from neighbors and making them accountable only to the desire or greed of the owner. For Christians sharing neighborhoods with one another, our work should be to refashion the commons. This can be something as simple as tearing down the privacy fence that divides your yard from your neighbor's so that it is easier to go back and forth between houses. Or it can be something more complex. For those with a mind and the skill for such things, it could mean creating community garden space with sitting areas and ample room for people to encounter one another and to enjoy the natural beauty that their own land is able to sustain. More prosaically, it could mean simply hosting neighbors regularly for dinner, creating spaces in which relationships can begin to form and be strengthened.

We live now on the other side of what Paul Kingsnorth has called "the great unsettling," and the only way back to healthy common living is the restoring of the commons, the reseeding of the gardens from which human community grows and is sustained. We have lived in a time of uprooting, and now it is for us to begin the work of becoming rooted again. Because the Christian church is being tutored in the school of Christian discipleship, trained by divine revelation to behold reality as it is and to love the world as God has made it to be, we are uniquely positioned to begin this work and to commend it to others.

The soil for this reseeding of the world is an encounter with divine grace, which is to say an encounter with our own inadequacy. Friedrich Nietzsche looks at each of us and says, "Take, achieve, make a name for yourself that will echo in eternity." What many of us are discovering is that this work is thankless and impossible, even for the most powerful among us. At best, we will be like Ozymandias, the great king remembered in Percy Shelley's poem of the same name—memorialized in a toppled-over statue, lost in endless dunes of sand. "Look on my works, ye mighty, and despair," we say. And yet,

> Nothing beside remains. Round the decay
> Of that colossal wreck, boundless and bare
> The lone and level sands stretch far away.[11]

Any person well acquainted with themselves knows we are not up to the task Nietzsche sets for us. And so we come back to Christianity, to the reality of our weakness and the need for grace so that we can be restored to life. Nietzsche's world has given us the machine. Jesus offers to us the cross—and the empty tomb. And in that empty tomb we see hope for a world renewed.

The first seeds of the world to come have been sown already in the garden where that tomb is found. They were planted on Easter morning when Christ, who was mistaken for the gardener, emerged from the tomb in triumph, casting down sin and Satan and restoring the possibility of a good life on a good earth before the face of a good God. We live still before his face now, and we turn our eyes out onto that good earth "whose astonishments we can never exhaust." God, who is himself a lover of life, speaks to us still, saying, "breathe, live, create," and he promises to give us all that we need to do that work.

It is time for us to begin.

ACKNOWLEDGMENTS

Thank you to the Ingram and Lamb families for being faithful, generous neighbors, and to Emma Noel for helping with childcare and housework while I was writing this book.

Thank you, once again, to Don Gates, my agent, and to Ethan McCarthy and everyone at IVP for their work to bring this book to publication.

Thank you to the community of Zion Church. Thanks especially to our pastors there, Stu Kerns and Keith Ghormley. After witnessing so much craziness at other churches throughout 2020, I will never again take mature, sensible spiritual leadership for granted. Thank you.

Thank you to the Benne.

Thank you to the *Mere Orthodoxy* editors and writers. Thanks especially for being unimpressed by me and for your persistent willingness to tell me when I'm being a fool—which is often.

Thank you to my colaborers at the Davenant Institute and Plough Publishing House.

Thank you to Rob and Ruth Meador, who provided the soil in which a love for God could take root.

Thank you to my children, Davy Joy, Wendell, Austin, and Ambrose, for your patience as Daddy wrote another book.

Thanks, most of all, to my wife, Joie. I suspect that the only way to know how hard it is to write a book is to have written one. And the only way to know how all-consuming and exhausting writing a book can be is to be married to an author. I am yours, my dearest friend, with much gratitude and joy.

NOTES

FOREWORD
[1]Wendell Berry, *Essays: 1969–1990* (New York: The Modern Library, 2019), 335.
[2]Berry, *Essays*, 337.

INTRODUCTION
Whole Life Politics at the End of the World
[1]"How a Listowel Priest Helped Dismantle Apartheid," Radio Kerry, April 3, 2020, www.radiokerry.ie/podcasts/kerry-today/listowel-priest-helped-dismantle-apartheid-south-africa-april-3rd-2020-212046.
[2]Frederick Douglass, *Narrative of the Life of Frederick Douglass* (New York: Barnes and Noble Classics, 2003), 100.
[3]Wendell Berry, *The Hidden Wound* (Berkeley, CA: North Point, 1989), 16-17.
[4]Herman Bavinck, *The Christian Worldview*, trans. and ed. Nathaniel Gray Sutanto, James Eglinton, and Cory C. Brock (Wheaton, IL: Crossway, 2019), 101.
[5]Martin Bucer, *Melanchthon and Bucer* (Philadelphia: Westminster, 1969), 257.

1 AN IMMENSE INHERITANCE
A Christian Account of Nature
[1]Gerard Manley Hopkins, "God's Grandeur," available at www.poetryfoundation.org/poems/44395/gods-grandeur.
[2]Emil Brunner, *The Divine Imperative* (Philadelphia: Westminster, 1937), 239.
[3]Pope John Paul II, "Evangelium Vitae," March 25, 1995, www.vatican.va/content/john-paul-ii/en/encyclicals/documents/hf_jp-ii_enc_25031995_evangelium-vitae.html.
[4]Paul Griffiths, *Intellectual Appetites* (Washington, DC: Catholic University of America Press, 2009), 43, 45.
[5]Hartmut Rosa, *The Uncontrollability of the World* (Medford, MA: Polity, 2020).
[6]Herman Bavinck, *The Christian Worldview*, trans. and ed. Nathaniel Gray Sutanto, James Eglinton, and Cory C. Brock (Wheaton, IL: Crossway, 2019), 23.
[7]James Eglinton, *Bavinck: A Critical Biography* (Grand Rapids, MI: Baker Academic, 2020), 226.

[8]Alfred Tennyson, "In Memoriam A. H. H." (1850), available at www.online -literature.com/tennyson/718/.

[9]Herman Bavinck, *Christian Worldview*, 109.

[10]Pope Benedict XVI, "If You Want to Cultivate Peace, Protect Creation," January 1, 2010, www.vatican.va/content/benedict-xvi/en/messages/peace/documents/hf_ben -xvi_mes_20091208_xliii-world-day-peace.html.

[11]John Webster, "'Love Is Also a Lover of Life': Creatio Ex Nihilo and Creaturely Goodness," *Modern Theology* 29, no. 2 (April 2013), 168.

[12]John Webster, *Christ Our Salvation* (Bellingham, WA: Lexham, 2020), 9.

2 THE GREAT UPROOTING
Race and the End of Nature

[1]Hannah Arendt, *The Human Condition* (Chicago: University of Chicago Press, 2018), 1.

[2]Quoted in Matthew Dickerson, "Wendell Berry, C. S. Lewis, J. R. R. Tolkien and the Dangers of a Technological Mindset," *Flourish Magazine*, Fall 2010, www.flourishonline .org/2010/12/wendell-berry-cs-lewis-jrr-tolkien-and-the-dangers-of-a-technological -mindset/.

[3]Emil Brunner, *The Divine Imperative* (Philadelphia: Westminster, 1937), 296.

[4]Quoted in Harold Raley, "Julian Marias: Philosopher of the Person," *Mere Orthodoxy*, October 2, 2019, https://mereorthodoxy.com/julian-marias/.

[5]Herman Bavinck, *The Christian Worldview*, trans. and ed. Nathaniel Gray Sutanto, James Eglinton, and Cory C. Brock (Wheaton, IL: Crossway, 2019), 67.

[6]Quoted in Willie James Jennings, *The Christian Imagination: Theology and the Origins of Race* (New Haven, CT: Yale University Press, 2010), 84.

[7]Willie James Jennings, "Can 'White' People Be Saved?," in *Can 'White' People Be Saved?*, ed. Love L. Sechrest, Johnny Ramírez-Johnson, and Amos Yong (Downers Grove, IL: InterVarsity Press, 2018), 30.

[8]Jennings, *Christian Imagination*, 83.

[9]Quoted in Jennings, *Christian Imagination*, 31.

[10]J. R. R. Tolkien, "Address to Admirers in Rotterdam," March 1958, recording available on YouTube, www.youtube.com/watch?v=7g5npSwWMsw.

[11]Jennings, *Christian Imagination*, 43.

[12]Jennings, *Christian Imagination*, 64.

[13]Quoted in Jennings, *Christian Imagination*, 61.

[14]Anne Fremantle, "On the Battleground of Faith, Their Weapon is Charity," *New York Times*, June 2, 1957, 243.

[15]"Nixon Aids Inuguration of New Nation, Ghana," *Los Angeles Times*, March 7, 1957, 11.

[16]Quoted in Mark Charles and Soong-Chan Rah, *Unsettling Truths: The Ongoing, Dehumanizing Legacy of the Doctrine of Discovery* (Downers Grove, IL: InterVarsity Press, 2019), 120.

[17]James Eglinton, *Bavinck: A Critical Biography* (Grand Rapids, MI: Baker Academic, 2020), 258.

[18]Simone Weil, "The Iliad, or the Poem of Force" (1945), https://theanarchistlibrary .org/library/simone-weil-the-iliad.

[19]Mark Jones, *Faith, Hope, Love: The Christ-Centered Way to Grow in Grace* (Wheaton, IL: Crossway, 2017), 23.

[20]Herman Bavinck, *Reformed Dogmatics*, trans. John Vriend, ed. John Bolt (Grand Rapids, MI: Baker, 2008), 1:301.

[21]Pope John Paul II, "Evangelium Vitae," March 25, 1995, www.vatican.va/content/john -paul-ii/en/encyclicals/documents/hf_jp-ii_enc_25031995_evangelium-vitae.html.

[22]C. S. Lewis, *The Last Battle* (New York: Harper Collins, 2000), 168.

3 THE UNMAKING OF PLACES

The Fruit of Industrialism

[1]J. Weston Phippen, "The Buffalo Killers," *The Atlantic*, May 13, 2016, www.theatlantic .com/national/archive/2016/05/the-buffalo-killers/482349/.

[2]*Ten Days on the Plains* (Crocker and Co., 1871), https://codyarchive.org/texts/wfc .bks00008.html.

[3]Carolyn Merchant, *American Environmental History: An Introduction* (New York: Columbia University Press, 2007).

[4]Nebraska Public Media, "Return of the American Bison," YouTube video, April 20, 2018, www.youtube.com/watch?v=Ww3cMgFr2xQ.

[5]Martin Meredith, *The Fate of Africa* (New York: Public Affairs, 2011), 2.

[6]J. R. R. Tolkien, *The Fellowship of the Ring* (New York: Ballantine, 1954), 34.

[7]Christopher Dawson, *Enquiries into Religion and Culture* (Washington, DC: Catholic University of America Press, 2009), 43.

[8]Dawson, *Enquiries into Religion and Culture*, 43.

[9]J. Gresham Machen, *Christianity and Liberalism* (Grand Rapids, MI: Eerdmans, 2009), 8.

[10]Kirkpatrick Sale, *Rebels Against the Future* (New York: Basic, 1996), 52.

[11]Sale, *Rebels Against the Future*, 32.

[12]Romano Guardini, *Letters from Lake Como* (Grand Rapids, MI: Eerdmans, 1994), 12.

[13]Andy Crouch, "An Invitation to Join the Tech-Wise Family Challenge," January 7, 2019, www.barna.com/techwisechallenge-andy-crouch/.

[14]Guardini, *Letters from Lake Como*, 13.

[15]Sale, *Rebels Against the Future*, 59.

4 THE UNMAKING OF THE BODY
Considering the Sexual Revolution

[1]Martha Marsh, "How Puerto Rican Women Were Used to Test the Birth Control Pill," *Medium*, May 17, 2017, https://medium.com/the-lily/how-puerto-rican-women-were-used-to-test-the-birth-control-pill-7453a3b6ab73.

[2]Bryony McNeill, "Freer Sex and Family Planning: A Short History of the Contraceptive Pill," *The Conversation*, May 13, 2018, https://theconversation.com/freer-sex-and-family-planning-a-short-history-of-the-contraceptive-pill-92282.

[3]Harriet A. Washington, *Medical Apartheid* (New York: Anchor, 2008).

[4]It wasn't just women that they tested the drug on either. Gregory Pincus, one of the main scientists to work on the drug, also experimented on mentally ill male patients, wondering if perhaps the drug could lower their testosterone levels, thereby making it harder for them to reproduce.

[5]Jennifer Worth, *Call the Midwife* (New York: Penguin, 2002), 5.

[6]Jonathan Chait, "Why Conservatives Use Novels to Justify Inequality," *Intelligencer*, May 8, 2015, https://nymag.com/intelligencer/2015/05/conservatives-use-novels-to-justify-inequality.html.

[7]John Heidenry, *What Wild Ecstasy* (New York: Simon & Schuster, 1997), 12.

[8]William Blake, "The Chimney Sweeper," available at www.poetryfoundation.org/poems/43654/the-chimney-sweeper-when-my-mother-died-i-was-very-young.

[9]Betty Friedan, *The Feminine Mystique* (New York: Norton, 2001), 1.

[10]Kyle Harper, *From Shame to Sin* (Cambridge, MA: Harvard University Press, 2013), 27.

[11]Presbyterian Church in America, "Ad Interim Committee Report on Human Sexuality," May 2020, https://pcaga.org/wp-content/uploads/2020/05/AIC-Report-to-48th-GA-5-28-20-1.pdf.

[12]"Presbyterian Church in America, "Report of the Ad Interim Committee on Human Sexuality," 39-40.

[13]Ross Douthat, "The Redistribution of Sex," *New York Times*, May 2, 2018, www.nytimes.com/2018/05/02/opinion/incels-sex-robots-redistribution.html.

5 THE UNMAKING OF THE REAL
Wonder Among the Institutions

[1]*The Meaning of Life*, directed by Terry Jones (London: Celandine Films, 1983).

[2]*The Book of Common Prayer*, "The Third Collect for Aid Against All Perils," www.churchofengland.org/prayer-and-worship/worship-texts-and-resources/book-common-prayer/order-evening-prayer.

[3]Ivan Illich, *The Convivial Society* (New York: Harper & Row, 1973), 7.

[4]Chimamanda Ngozi Adichie, "The Danger of a Single Story," TEDGlobal 2009, www.ted.com/talks/chimamanda_ngozi_adichie_the_danger_of_a_single_story/transcript?language=en.

[5]Wendell Berry, "How to Be a Poet," www.poetryfoundation.org/poetrymagazine/poems/41087/how-to-be-a-poet.

[6]Alexander Solzhenitsyn, "A World Split Apart," delivered June 8, 1978, at Harvard University, Cambridge, MA, www.americanrhetoric.com/speeches/alexander solzhenitsynharvard.htm.

6 AGAINST THE REVOLUTION
The Beginnings of Christian Social Doctrine

[1]Amy Nelson Burnett, *The Yoke of Christ* (Ann Arbor, MI: Truman State University Press, 1994).

[2]Martin Bucer, *Instructions in Christian Love* (Eugene, OR: Wipf & Stock), 22.

[3]Bucer, *Instructions in Christian Love*, 27.

[4]Bucer, *Instructions in Christian Love*, 39.

[5]Bucer, *Instructions in Christian Love*, 40.

[6]Bucer, *Instructions in Christian Love*, 42.

[7]Quoted in Susannah Black, "Sealed in Blood: Aristopopulism and the City of Man," *Mere Orthodoxy*, March 19, 2019, https://mereorthodoxy.com/sealed-in-blood-aristopopulism-and-the-city-of-man/.

[8]Herman Bavinck, *The Christian Worldview*, trans. and ed. Nathaniel Gray Sutanto, James Eglinton, and Cory C. Brock (Wheaton, IL: Crossway, 2019), 22.

[9]James Davison Hunter, *To Change the World* (New York: Oxford University Press, 2010), 213.

[10]Johnny Walsh, "Nadia Bolz-Weber Does Ministry Differently," *Out in Jersey*, October 21, 2018, https://outinjersey.net/nadia-bolz-weber-does-ministry-differently/.

[11]Herman Bavinck, "The Catholicity of Christianity and the Church," https://bavinck.files.wordpress.com/2017/05/bavinck-catholicity.pdf, 221.

[12]Bavinck, "Catholicity of Christianity," n. 3.

7 THE EARTH IS OUR MOTHER
On Christianity, Land, and Animals

[1]Johannes Meier, "Beating the Big Dry," *Plough Quarterly*, May 6, 2019, www.plough.com/en/topics/justice/environment/beating-the-big-dry.

[2]Pope Francis, "Laudato Si," May 24, 2015, www.vatican.va/content/francesco/en/encyclicals/documents/papa-francesco_20150524_enciclica-laudato-si.html.

[3]Jonathan Edwards, "The Nakedness of Job," in *The Works of Jonathan Edwards*, vol. 10 (New Haven, CT: Yale University Press), 406, available at edwards.yale.edu.

[4]Pope John Paul II, "Evangelium Vitae," March 25, 1995, www.vatican.va/content/john-paul-ii/en/encyclicals/documents/hf_jp-ii_enc_25031995_evangelium-vitae.html.

[5]C. S. Lewis, *The Lion, the Witch, and the Wardrobe* (New York: Harper Collins, 2005), 123.

[6]John Piper, "Clyde Kilby's Resolutions for Mental Health and for Staying Alive to God in Nature," *Desiring God*, August 27, 1990, www.desiringgod.org/articles/clyde-kilbys-resolutions-for-mental-health-and-for-staying-alive-to-god-in-nature.

[7]Pope Francis, "Laudato Si," May 24, 2015, www.vatican.va/content/francesco/en/encyclicals/documents/papa-francesco_20150524_enciclica-laudato-si.html.

[8]Enric Sala, *The Nature of Nature* (Washington, DC: National Geographic Partners, 2020), 71.

[9]Barbara Cooney, *Miss Rumphius* (New York: Puffin, 1985).

[10]Meier, "Beating the Big Dry."

[11]Meier, "Beating the Big Dry."

8 A VISION OF CHRISTIAN BELONGING
The Household and the Sexual Revolution

[1]Today Strasbourg is part of France, but in the sixteenth century it was a German-speaking city belonging to the Holy Roman Empire.

[2]Quoted in Herman Selderhuis, *Marriage and Divorce in the Thought of Martin Bucer* (Kirksville, MO: Thomas Jefferson University Press, 1999).

[3]Christopher Lasch, *Haven in a Heartless World* (New York: Norton, 1995).

[4]Quoted in Nancy Pearcey, *Total Truth* (Wheaton, IL: Crossway, 2008), 333.

[5]Pope Benedict XVI, "The Human Family: A Community of Peace," January 1, 2008, www.vatican.va/content/benedict-xvi/en/messages/peace/documents/hf_ben-xvi_mes_20071208_xli-world-day-peace.html.

[6]Martin Bucer, *Melanchthon and Bucer* (Philadelphia: Westminster, 1969), 327.

[7]Matthew Lee Anderson, "The Christian Sexual Ethic (for High Schoolers)," *The Path Before Us*, July 27, 2020, www.getrevue.co/profile/matthewleeanderson/issues/the-christian-sexual-ethic-for-high-schoolers-issue-204-266193.

[8]Andrew Willard Jones, "What States Can't Do," *New Polity*, July 24, 2020.

[9]See, for example, St. Gregory of Nyssa, "On Virginity," www.newadvent.org/fathers/2907.htm; St. Clement, "Two Epistles on Virginity," www.newadvent.org/fathers/0803.htm; St. Ambrose, "Concerning Virginity," www.newadvent.org/fathers/3407.htm; and St. Augustine, "Of Holy Virginity," www.newadvent.org/fathers/1310.htm.

[10]St. Ambrose, "Concerning Virginity."

9 THE WORLD IN CRACKED ICONS
Wonder, Death, and the End of All Things

[1]Thomas Watson, *All Things for Good* (Edinburgh: Banner of Truth Trust, 1986), 32.

[2]G. K. Chesterton, *What Is Wrong with the World* (San Francisco: Ignatius, 1994), 194.

10 POLITICS BEYOND ACCOMPLISHMENT
Toward a Politics of Care

[1]Justin Hawkins, "Dignity Beyond Accomplishment," *Mere Orthodoxy*, January 19, 2021. https://mereorthodoxy.com/dignity-beyond-accomplishment/.

[2]J. M. Gustafson, "Mongolism, Parental Desires, and the Right to Life," *Perspectives in Biology and Medicine*, Summer 1973.

[3]Gustafson, "Mongolism."

[4]Sarah Zhang, "The Last Children of Down Syndrome," *The Atlantic*, December 2020, www.theatlantic.com/magazine/archive/2020/12/the-last-children-of-down-syndrome/616928/.

[5]Stanley Hauerwas, "Why Community is Dangerous," *Plough*, May 19, 2016, www.plough.com/en/topics/community/church-community/why-community-is-dangerous.

[6]John Winthrop, "A Model of Christian Charity," posted by Frank Viola on *The Deeper Journey* (blog), March 11, 2021, www.patheos.com/blogs/frankviola/johnwinthrop/.

[7]Winthrop, "A Model of Christian Charity."

[8]John Calvin, quoted in Marilynne Robinson, "Open Thy Hand Wide," in *When I Was a Child I Read Books* (New York: Picador, 2013), 77-78.

[9]Anne Helen Petersen, "The Errand Friend," *Culture Study*, January 17, 2021, https://annehelen.substack.com/p/the-errand-friend.

[10]Willie James Jennings, *The Christian Imagination: Theology and the Origins of Race* (New Haven, CT: Yale University Press, 2010), 59.

[11]Percy Shelley, "Ozymandias," www.poetryfoundation.org/poems/46565/ozymandias.

ALSO BY JAKE MEADOR

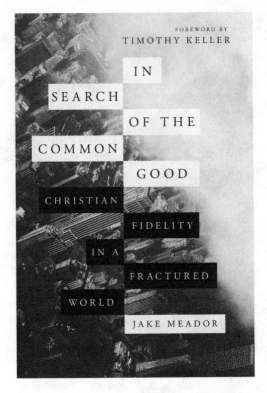

In Search of the Common Good
978-0-8308-4554-5